CREATION, REVELATION, AND PHILOSOPHY

CREATION, REVELATION, AND PHILOSOPHY

Johan Mekkes

Dordt College Press

Cover design by Scott Vande Kraats
Layout by Carla Goslinga

Copyright © 2010 by Chris van Haeften

Unless noted otherwise, all Scripture quotations are taken from the HOLY BIBLE: NEW INTERNATIONAL VERSION®. NIV®. Copyright © 1973, 1978, 1984 by International Bible Society. Used by permission of Zondervan Publishing House. All rights reserved.

Fragmentary portions of this book may be freely used by those who are interested in sharing this author's insights and observations, so long as the material is not pirated for monetary gain and so long as proper credit is visibly given to the publisher, the author, and the translator. Others, and those who wish to use larger sections of text, must seek written permission from the publisher.

Printed in the United States of America.

Dordt College Press   www.dordt.edu/dordt_press
498 Fourth Avenue NE
Sioux Center, Iowa 51250
United States of America

Library of Congress Cataloging-in-Publication Data

Mekkes, J. P. A.
 [Scheppingsopenbaring en wijsbegeerte. English]
 Creation, revelation, and philosophy / Johan Mekkes ; translated by Chris van Haeften.
     p. cm.
  ISBN 978-0-932914-83-5 (pbk. : alk. paper)
 1. Christianity--Philosophy. 2. Heidegger, Martin, 1889-1976. 3. Jaspers, Karl, 1883-1969. 4. Sartre, Jean-Paul, 1905-1980. I. Title.
   BR100.M37613 2010
   230.01--dc22
                         2010003418

ISBN 978-0-932914-83-5

CONTENTS

Preface i

Introduction iii

1. Introduction. The Limits of Philosophy 1

2. Truth and Ground-Motive 17

3. Revelation and Listening 23

4. Philosophy and Theology 33

5. Creation and Pseudo-Revelation 41

6. The Word: Revelation and the Fall 45

7. The Dynamics and Motive of
   Philosophical Reflection 49

8. The "Common Grace" Hypothesis, the Archimedean
   Point, and the Antithesis 57

9. Perspective on the Limits of Temporal Existence 69

10. History and the Dynamics of Disclosure 75

Author's Preface

This study does not pretend to say anything that could not, partly or in a different manner, have been said elsewhere. It originated from the encounter with the basic questions of our times in the academic teaching at the "front" of the Foundation for Calvinistic Philosophy in The Netherlands. The sole responsibility for it remains with the writer.

It presupposes an acquaintance with the philosophy of the cosmonomic idea. Twenty-five years after the origination of this philosophy, the attempt is made here to penetrate to the mutual grounds in philosophy and present-day movements, which have step by step become clearer.

Fall 1960

Translator's Preface

This book was first published in Dutch under the title *Scheppingsopenbaring en wijsbegeerte* in 1961. That is a long time ago. Yet I thought it worthwhile to translate it. For even though from a historical point of view Mekkes's discussions of Heidegger, Jaspers, and Sartre may seem outdated, they yet serve to bring out the radical and dynamic nature of Christian philosophy. And this dynamics is of all times.

I took up the task of translating this work upon request from my friend Albert Gedraitis. It has been an arduous task. Mekkes adopts a style of his own. Trained as a jurist, and versed in the languages of Continental philosophy, his Dutch language is, moreover, somewhat archaic. Johan van der Hoeven considers this book a pearl, but it is, according to him, a pearl in a shell. I agree with him, and I hope that my attempt to unpack Mekkes's long and complicated sentences into readable English will make this pearl more accessible. For it seems to me that this book is an impressive reference to the pearl of great price referred to in the Gospel of Matthew.

I am very much obliged to the editorial work done by Bruce C. Wearne. Without his creative effort to change my Netherlish into a more refined language, the result would have been a far cry from what the reader finds here. I also wish to thank Roger Henderson for his help in understanding the exact meaning of some of Mekkes's puzzling formulations.

Chris van Haeften, February 2009

Introduction

Johan Peter Albertus Mekkes was born in Harderwijk in 1898. In 1987 in his 89th year he died in The Hague. From 1915 he was enlisted in the army of the Netherlands, and became an officer in 1920. From 1942 to 1945 the Germans made him a prisoner of war. In 1945 he left the army, to work for the Dutch government. During the period 1932–1935, he studied law at the Catholic University, Nijmegen. And in April 1940, just three weeks before the Germans occupied the Netherlands, he obtained a doctor's degree at the Vrije Universiteit in Amsterdam. Under the direction of Herman Dooyeweerd, he submitted a voluminous thesis on the development of the humanistic theories of the law state.

In 1947 he was appointed as lecturer of Calvinistic philosophy at the Netherlands School of Economics, which in 1973 became part of the Erasmus University in Rotterdam. By 1972, however, he had left because of retirement. From 1949 to 1970 he was visiting professor of Calvinistic philosophy at the University of Leiden. From 1963 to 1970 he also lectured in a similar visiting capacity at Eindhoven Technical University. The Delft Technical University also saw him providing lectures for some years.

From 1955 to 1975 he taught philosophy and constitutional theory at the School for Higher Defense Studies. Behind the scenes, Mekkes was also active in the field of Christian politics, as a political party member.

From 1960 to 1968 Mekkes was a member of the editorial board of *Philosophia Reformata*, the academic journal of the Association for Reformational Philosophy. Preceding this position, he had, for many years, acted as secretary of the editorial board.

During his active life as a philosopher, from 1940 to 1980, Mekkes wrote four books and hundreds of articles and extended book reviews. In 1961 *Scheppingsopenbaring en wijsbegeerte* (Creation, Revelation, and Philosophy) appeared. His 1965 book *Teken en motief der creatuur* (Sign and Motive of Creation) contains an extended confrontation with the philosophy of Karl Jaspers. In 1966, an important article, entitled "Grondmotief" (Ground Motive), appeared in *Philosophia Reformata*. His 1971 book *Radix, tijd en kennen* (Radix, Time, and Knowing) can be considered as a discussion with Heidegger. His last book appeared in 1973. Under the title *Tijd der bezinning* (Time of Reflection) he discussed the mission of the movement for reformational philosophy. At the same time this booklet can be read as a reflection on his own path through philosophy. A somewhat different sort of reflection can be found in an article titled "De grenzen van het denken – een gesprek" (The boundaries of thinking – a discussion) (*Radix* 4, 1978, 55–65), which actually extends a mail discussion between Mekkes and myself.

With some exceptions all of Mekkes's work is in Dutch. I therefore welcome the translation of his 1961 book, which is a good example of his way of philosophizing.

It was my privilege to attend his weekly lectures from 1964 to 1970. He did not teach us a philosophical system, but delivered philosophy *in actu*. In particular, he imposed upon his students an awareness of all attempts to transgress, by reason or otherwise, the boundaries set by time and the human condition. Put otherwise, his was a critical attitude towards all human attempts to deliver, from some alleged God's-eye point-of-view, the answer to all questions.

Standing in the tradition of the philosophy of the cosmonomic idea, Mekkes had his own distinct voice. Guided by the method of transcendental critique, he ventured into discussions with Heidegger, Sartre, and Jaspers, to name the great philosophers of his age. It is good that, finally, the English-speaking world can learn more about a remarkable, albeit very modest, philosopher.

Bert M. Balk
Rotterdam, 18 July 2009

1.

INTRODUCTION.
THE LIMITS OF PHILOSOPHY

The question about the limits of philosophy is highly controversial. It is already complicated by its connection to the question about the limits of scientific theory. Let us make it clear, right from the start of our investigation, that it is not our intention to enter into a discussion about the possibility of *pure* theoretical philosophy. I will frankly admit that I do not know what can be meant by the term *pure* in the phrase "pure theory." After all, even though scientific theory is concerned with everything in our existence, it is nevertheless itself but one sector of our life. Our theoretical activity can only arise from within this life, and its systematization is a matter of recurrent activity by living people.

Therefore, to pretend that science can be "pure" might seem a dogmatic "stain." This is not to say that we would blame anyone for such pretension. We simply do not concede the possibility of any such "purity," and therefore we are not taking aim at those who hold the opposite view. Hopefully, it will become clear that our subsequent discussions imply our respect for this claim that we have to reject.

Today, philosophy occupies one of the domains ascribed to scientific theory. This raises the question of its place and its content. And although we have to reject the possibility of a "pure" theoretical philosophy, we still have to deal with the problem of identifying the limits of philosophy and of scientific theory. That is to say, we have to investigate whether a transgression of the limits of theoretical thinking is, in itself, a transgression of the limits of philosophy.

This question cannot be discussed in a purely abstract manner. Philosophy, as it presents itself to us, is a part of concrete human life. It responds to the needs of human life, and it proceeds within the possibilities of this life, within a given historical development. This development can be surveyed in retrospect, but it could never have been predetermined from any point of view. Moreover, philosophy as we know it is a product of the particular development of Western "culture."

Within this frame, and up until the present time, philosophy has been understood as the attempt to give a rational account for, and answer to, the ultimate questions. This characterization of its task has persisted, even after philosophy could leave the investigation of the special areas of life to the special sciences.

If it were objected that philosophy should abstain from such ultimate questions, and that only in that way it can still make an acceptable contribution, then, by this very proposal, the final philosophical question would have been answered. The formulation of all consequent problems would result from, and continue to refer to, this definitive starting point.

Our problem, therefore, will be: What *is* the nature of a responsible answer to, and an account of, the ultimate questions? Can this account be theoretical in nature?

By merely rejecting the possibility of a purely theoretical philosophy in general terms, we have not fully decided yet about the competence of philosophy as such. No matter from which side we approach this problem, the final question will always come down to this: how will philosophy refer to the ultimate unity of reality in its entirety? That is to say, how will it refer to the domain of all human activities and experiences, including those associated with the entire range of theoretical activity, in a unified, non-contradictory way?

There is an implication in the way these questions are framed that will be readily countered by the observation that contemporary man, insofar as he still wants to pay any attention at all to the pretensions of philosophy, will surely not want to be bothered by the ancient notion of a unity of being. After all, he is only interested in *praxis*, in what is at hand, in the efficient handling of what can be grasped. Therefore, if he raises any questions concerning truth and value, he does so for practical reasons. And if a reference to some unity appears necessary, as with a set of axioms, then he will only deal with these questions in terms of the *plurality* that is supposed to guarantee the mutual relativity of all possible pproaches. On this standpoint, each "basic" attitude can be pragmatically accepted, only if it serves to contribute to the practical results of science.

However, this readily-assumed position about plurality in fact springs from a specific basic attitude. *This* attitude does not allow for any other fundamental possibility. The thesis of plurality cannot tolerate the right of any other basic attitude. That is to say that with respect to the problem of unity there has been no escape, neither from the question nor

Introduction. The Limits of Philosophy

from an answer. In this way a definite position regarding unity has been taken, as was inevitable.

This indicates a new problem,[1] closely connected with the question of the possible coincidence of the limits of theory and philosophy. It plays a critical role, not only within science and philosophy, but throughout Western culture.

This problem is reflected in some recent developments. Alongside the persistent pragmatic attitude in thought and action, there is an apparent interest to "overcome existentialism." And it is presumed that there is a radical antithesis between consistent existentialism and any "philosophy of ambiguity." And, occasioned by this, a comprehensive critique of dialectical thought in philosophy and action has been undertaken.[2]

These developments show that the restriction of philosophical analysis to the "data" of "the world" has taken its toll. Phenomenological reduction is no longer considered a secure starting point for freedom of inquiry, nor as its safe and ultimate refuge. It seems as if it is felt necessary to abandon one's own territory in order to enter into free commerce with the enemy. At the same time, the philosophy of the great Karl Jaspers with its ambiguous flight into transcendence, is ridiculed as a last, but significant, expression of the "descending class" (*classe descendante*).

If ever there were a time to begin a search for an answer to the questions about the character and fundamental unity of philosophy, then it is today. The question is: where do we have to look in order to begin to understand? This question is complicated by the fact that philosophy already presupposes the theoretical attitude. Therefore, we have no choice but to start from the *theoretical* attitude of *thinking*. Philosophy derives its meaning from referring to the whole of human life as a unity. In this way it is directed towards the ultimate questions. But it starts from the theoretical attitude of thought.

Is this thesis true? Can it mean that, in a historical sense, philosophy began in this way? Obviously not. It was only after its initial first steps that Western reflection consolidated itself into "rational" reflection. And

---

1   Namely, of the rationality of the philosopher. This problem appears to touch on the rationality of philosophy and on the relation between the philosopher and his philosophy [tr.].

2   Translator's note: Mekkes is pointing here to Heidegger's later philosophy and to Sartre's *Critique of Dialectical Reason*. These works show a renewed interest in the limits of philosophy, and can be interpreted as a qualification of the existentialist opposition against pragmatism. See Johan van der Hoeven, *The Rise and Development of the Phenomenological Movement*, Lecture 3. Christian Perspectives Series ARSS, Hamilton, Ontario 1965.

no matter what battles have subsequently been fought over the pros and cons of metaphysics, these battles have, without exception, been fought on the basis of a deeply-felt obligation that they should be accounted for rationally. The manner in which this has been done can rightfully be criticized from any number of angles. Such criticism has been given, in most cases with the aim of winning the main battle. However, with the progress of scientific method and the sharp delineation of the mutual lines for battle, compliance with the standard that philosophy be rational is surely required. The only question is, what is the range of this standard? An answer to *this* preliminary question is surely *legitimate*. It should not be rebuked for falling short of the norm of rationality.

That is to say, the intended answer must meet the standard in so far as it is valid. The remaining question will be whether the dispute about the range of the standard will come within the range of that standard itself. In other words, does not he who thinks that the end of the discussion coincides with the end of rationality, *eo ipso* violate his norm, thus fundamentally abandoning his own position?

Today it is a historical *given* that philosophy, after winning fame within Western culture, does start out from the theoretical attitude of thought. This fact of theoretical practice is known as the practice of theoretically abstracting and opposing two poles, the subject and the object. The philosophical battlefield is openly or covertly dominated by questions concerning their meaning and mutual position.

Pre-critical thought, in dealing with the theoretical "Gegenstand,"[3] has either revealed one of these poles, or tried to make a theoretically oppositional "substance" out of both of them. Critical idealism attempted to synthesize both under the dominion of the subjective idea of reason. Today these two movements have definitively parted company. However, they cannot completely let go of each other. Through this interdependent divorce they give expression to an ongoing crisis. The limit of philosophy is now sharply marked out by this crisis, precisely because, while originating foremost from within philosophical thought, it is now, in its own way, penetrating and influencing the theoretical domain from the outside.

We have shown that thought that is exclusively oriented to objectivity and praxis, and that recognizes no further unity than that of an "axiomatic system," continued for that reason to refer to a plurality of possible approaches. We indicated that, in spite of itself, it remained wed-

---

3 German for "that which stands over against" something else: in this case that which results from the theoretical abstractive oppositioning [tr.].

ded to the *unity* of *this* (subjective) standpoint. On the other hand, the turn to the pole of "subjectivity" in the dialectical systematics of phenomenological existentialist thought remains bound to "objectivity," to the "world," to the "in-itself."

The mutual tension between these two streams is mainly felt within the latter, because the former is hardly interested in philosophical tensions. It is the tension of the living world of Western culture. On the one hand, we find the rational urge for control, which has characterized the Humanistic basic principle that leads the way in this culture. On the other hand, we find the reflection on the sovereignty of this human freedom itself, from which this urge for control continues to originate.

As we have noted, in recent years there has been an attempt to reconcile these two basic tendencies.[4] However, without success. On the contrary, because of its fundamental extra-philosophical nature, the tension between them has appeared again in the sharpest light. This puts the problem of the limits of theoretical philosophy in a peculiar contemporary perspective.

What actually is the meaning of these contending poles, which dominate the opposition in contemporary philosophy? They are the poles of some dialectic between subject and object. Where does this dialectic come from, and by what right does it make its appearance in philosophy?

For a brief explanation we turn to the beginnings of Western "rational" reflection in philosophy. It was man who thought about beings and their Being. He set himself over against Being in his *theoretical* reflection. Naturally, in his reflection he reserved a place for himself among all beings. Nevertheless, in doing so, he still maintained his actual reflecting position. No doubt he was aware of the peculiarity of this, even as he was aware of the imperfections of his thinking, its dependence on his body, and so forth. Thus he found it necessary to form an idea of what perfect thinking would be like. To this perfect thought he ascribed the status of divinity. At the same time, this divine perfection remained the product of, and dependent upon, the actual reflection of the philosopher himself. This marks the inception of a conflict, of which the philosophers could hardly become conscious as long as they remained focused merely on the product of their reflections.

Western philosophy has proceeded along the lines of this basic pattern. On the one hand, there was rational thinking, which was supposed to give the answer, even the ultimate answer, to all questions; on the other hand, there was the field of investigation for thought. This field was ra-

---

4 Mekkes refers to the mentioned attempt to overcome existentialism.

tionally conceived and embraced all beings, including god and thinking men.

While in the course of time mythological and speculative contaminations gradually disappeared, thought acquired the position of last court of appeal. There was no appeal beyond its "rational" judgment. The only thing that mattered was to think purely. This was to be the ground upon which the philosophical and theoretical tournament would be played out. In the meantime, reality continued, in some form or other, to offer resistance to the claims of reason. This resistance became acute when, after the medieval disputes, Humanism appeared on the scene. Automatically, it took over the rational inheritance with its basic pattern, but it charged this pattern with a veritable dynamical content, namely the dynamics of the passion for control by the supposedly sovereign, free human personality.

From now on theoretical thought is increasingly made to serve the realization of this supposed sovereignty. Naturally, *thinking* can only promote this realization by, on the one hand, serving praxis and, on the other hand, by bringing this realization to consciousness in philosophical reflection. We have seen that these two aspects were initially held together in different forms of mutual tension, and that they have subsequently parted company and gone their separate ways.

On the one hand, the illusion of sovereignty continues to stimulate the pragmatistic-positivistic passion for control. Here it is deemed to be somehow below human dignity to pay explicit attention to this. Yet, on the other hand, Western man has become afraid of this state of affairs as he begins to reflect on the precariousness of his existence, all the while trying to save the supposed sovereignty of theoretical thought by means of some kind of "reason"-ing. First, following the lead of the philosophers, he thought of himself as thinking historically, or as bringing history into conscious thought. Nowadays, by means of phenomenological methods, he either seeks a privileged position for himself as a "presence" over against fixed "being" [Sartre, tr.]. Or again, he seeks a position in which he, clad with the cloak of prophecy, is being addressed by "Being" (now conceived as dynamical) [Heidegger, tr.]. Or, yet again, he seeks refuge by adopting an extremely irrational idea of reason, a reason that is expected to save him who is not merely rational but reasonable, from any failure in this broken netherworld and thus to elevate him above it [Jaspers, tr.].

Reason-ing can only find its desired status by contrasting it with its counter pole, the world. Man, in search of freedom, can never leave it behind. He lives in it, and only through it is he who he is. Thus, within this dynamic system, the old poles of Western thinking show themselves again in a new guise. As is presumed, however, on the one side we no longer have just an observer, but man in his supposedly historical totality, while on the other side not merely a field of investigation or intellectual objectivity, but a supposedly total field of experience.

Or so it is claimed. But the old problem remains, namely, the problem of the philosopher, who says so, and who does indeed assign to himself a place within his own system. Within this system he will meet, however, with difficulties that are highly significant for the kind of investigation we intend to carry out.

Having "liberated" itself from all belief, myth, and metaphysics, philosophical thought attempted to anchor itself in theoretical method. In so far as its main interests were, and are, the "objects" of the "world," it did not and does not think that it needs to give any account of its own position. After all, universally valid thought, if it aims for purity, *is* the last court of appeal.

Even philosophical reflection on "subjectivity" has acquiesced with this justification out of a fear of losing its reliability. By regarding this reflection as a province of some sort of general consciousness, as described in the systematics of the reflecting philosopher, he took a position that seemed not much more difficult than that of the purely objectifying philosopher.

However, he who for the sake of freedom makes an ultimate appeal to man's individual free existence has, by doing so, placed himself in an isolated position. Here he cannot avoid getting into conflict with the universality of communal thought. For whereas man and his "world," as well as their mutual correlation within the "system," appear to be admissible to the court of reason with a claim of universality, yet, in fact the philosopher would have to split himself in two; between a total person who cannot, and a philosopher who can, lay claim to such universality.

This situation caught the attention of the great and level-headed philosopher Karl Jaspers. He exercised his most noble philosophical abilities in trying to resolve this threatening antinomy. It will be sufficient to give a short exposition of his view in order to show how it illustrates our argument.

It is fashionable these days to speak of the teleological character of philosophic thought. It is supposed that such thought progressively approximates truth more and more over the course of history. This insight, though stamped by historicism, is certainly realistic as regards the increasingly acute and irresolvable contradictions resulting from the confession of sovereign reason. It was existentialism's task to yield this insight to "perennial philosophy."

The philosopher must inevitably run into the irresolvable conflict between his own historically moved and moving existence and the universality demanded from his philosophical assertions. Jaspers takes this conflict altogether seriously. If historical existence (absolutized and frozen by him in the idea of "transcendence") were to ever demand from him the repudiation of his entire philosophy, then this would indeed have to be done, he says. However, at that point, he does not acknowledge the antinomy that it is precisely this extremely individualized demand that would also have to be dropped. For it is presented as a *universal within* his philosophy, and only has validity because of that philosophy. Therefore, it would have to be dropped along with his philosophy. A discussion about such existential demands can, for Jaspers, only take place under the restraints of "reasonable" communication. He considers the rejection of these restraints as "Catholicism." Anyone who is guilty of this cannot be reasonably tolerated.

Even though, according to Jaspers, man only attains to reality in the experience of Being as it were by "shipwreck," he has not anticipated this shipwreck for his own philosophy. Heidegger is right when he writes that "There is a chasm between philosophizing about Shipwreck and thought that is being shipwrecked."

Sartre's *Critique of Dialectical Reason* accepts the consequence of Jaspers' conflict to some degree. It describes consciousness as always ahead of itself in its project. Nevertheless, this consciousness is, before all else, rational logicizing consciousness. As such it remains identical to itself, even though, at this moment of history, the rational universal validity of Sartre's philosophy has narrowed itself to the rational universality of Marxism. As soon as Marxism will have accepted existentialism as the human dimension, existentialism will have lost its specific *raison d'être*, and will by philosophical teleology have been cancelled as the basis of all inquiry. Each historicism has the inherent antinomy of universality that *needs to be surpassed*. Here this antinomy is squared at the cost of the (almost shamelessly) deeper antinomy of the *universal* validity of existentialistic Marxism projecting itself into history. In spite of its apparent contestation of the opposite, the pole of control has strengthened itself over against existentialism by means of the pragmatic intent (or even: *telos*) to be subservient to class consciousness.

It appears that the absolutization of theoretical thinking creates a tension and an internal antinomy by which philosophical "reason" is brought to its limits. By investigating some examples of this tension in existentialist thought we got these limits in view. In the attempts to transcend this tension the limits of philosophical thinking appeared to be transgressed. We saw this in Jaspers' opposition between rational communication and "Catholicism" and in Sartre's existence projecting into Marxism (or, earlier, into the *logos* of absurd freedom). Furthermore, we witnessed, in this transgression, the appearance of an irrational *trust* in reason. And finally, this trust appeared unable to be maintained when faced with the freedom demanded by the (philosophizing) "subject." It even appeared to stand in its way.

The standard of competent reason is violated in such transgressions. It loses its validity, and is henceforth only used for the structuring of an argument that has its origin somewhere else.

We cannot possibly make an objection to the fact that theory has a non-theoretical origin. This is a real state of affairs. That is why we wanted to do justice to the standpoint of the supposed plurality of objective truth. On that standpoint too, theoretical reasoning originates from a non-theoretical starting point, namely that it is not possible to ask questions beyond theory, while it is not possible for theoretical thought to reach higher than the (unity of) plurality. Before the court of truth this standpoint appeared to be exclusive. This is beyond our objections. But it may be demanded that such supra-theoretical origins be *recognized*. For our battle is fundamentally not an intra-philosophical discussion for the sake of discussion. The goal of the discussion is to show philosophy's limits, in order to bring to light what is ruled and decided from the outside about the inside.

Theoretical argumentation is carried out by means of "rationality." But in the West this "rationality" usurps the throne *from* which the argumentation starts. It is tacitly confessed to be the *pre*supposed, most original origin. Obviously, this must complicate the attempt to clarify the mutual positions. And this complication will camouflage the controversial limits. That gives us all the more reason to distinguish them carefully.

The "sign" by which this pretender is to be recognized is the hypostatization of the theoretical Gegenstand-relation. Taking theory for the origin *is* the violation of the standard of competent reason. Theoretical dialectic, with its logical subject-object relation (Gegenstand-relation), is put *in* the place of *the* origin.

This appears contestable. And indeed, alternative philosophical "origins" have been put forward from many different sides. They were called god, *intellectus archetypus*, self-producing spirit, or, more abstractly, ground of ground, existential *Ur-sprung*, adverting and averting Being, and so forth.

The relation between origin and theoretical dialectic becomes strikingly apparent in Sartre's *Critique of Dialectical Reason*. After showing the opposition between Hegel and Kierkegaard, Sartre says: "The truth is that subjectivity is neither everything nor nothing; it represents a moment in the objective process (that in which externality is internalized), and this moment is perpetually eliminated only to be perpetually reborn. Now, each of these ephemeral moments—which rise up in the course of human history and which are never either the first or the last—is lived as a *point of departure* by the subject of the history."[5] In the repeated encounter with the "objects" that arouse class-opposition, the subject becomes conscious of this opposition and inwardly transcends it. Thus his conscience becomes class-consciousness.

We see that the subject is conceived as a historically experiencing subject, while the object is the world for which this subject is struggling. This struggle is eminently practical, but is waged by the "conscious" subject, "which necessarily implies that we must develop a theory of consciousness." Throughout, Sartre fully emphasizes conscious conscience, the pre-reflexive cogito. In order to make true dialectical contact with the objects, without becoming rigid and dogmatic, we need a *theory* of knowledge as theoretical knowledge of this practical consciousness.

Pre-reflexive consciousness is no more than an abstraction from the full praxis of human subjectivity. Everything else is conceived as opposed to consciousness. At the same time, consciousness must be part of a dialectical praxis (namely as class-consciousness). Sartre is only able to achieve this at the cost of this antinomy: On the one hand, the subject is a historical moment of dialectical praxis, while on the other hand, the same subject as conscious subject of the (dialectical) theory of knowledge is claimed to have universal validity.

What really has been placed in the position of ultimate origin here is the theoretical *dialectic between* the sovereign (Marxist) *conscious conscience* of (anybody,[6] read:) the philosopher on the one hand, *and* its *Gegenstand*, namely the (historical) dialectic of the continuously projecting class-consciousness and the (economically-material) world of "objects,"

---

5   *The Search for Method* (1st. Part), *Introduction to a Critique of Dialectical Reason* 1960 (translated by Hazel Barnes), http://marxists.org/references/archive/sartre/works/critic/sartre1.htm

6   *"n'importe qui"*

Introduction. The Limits of Philosophy

on the other hand.

In line with the fundamental idea of all Humanistic philosophy, reason, as rational and therefore only valid sovereignty, places theoretical dialectic in the position of origin. In sovereign control it creates its own Gegenstand, the existentialist-Marxist dialectic. This origin rules the epistemological (i.c. Marxist) argumentation *from the outside*. It determines its *meaning*. Beyond this meaning-determination no appeal is possible.

It should not be objected that it is *class*-consciousness that is speaking here. There can be no objection to its manner of performance in the debate, as long as the theoretical rules of the game, which exclude the supra-theoretical idea of origin, are obeyed by all participants. For within the debate, the philosopher, as before, has used a strictly logical argumentation. So, the way in which he has carried out his program is beyond reproach: "The only theory of knowledge that can be valid today is one that is founded on that truth of micro-physics: the experimenter is part of the experimental system." The fact that this is taken as a basis for the narrowing of existentialism into a Marxist frame results indeed in a dialectical nuance in the tension in the origin-idea. But this is only a further reason why we should once again look at the *limits* of what is possible for theory.

The *fundamental* antinomy, we have repeatedly indicated, shows its logical side in the structure of the argumentation. Yet it integrally transcends the logical aspect, because of the two poles that at the same time presuppose and exclude each other. "Subjectivity" and "objectivity," as they figure in this internal philosophical dialectic, are merely two variable representations of this fundamental polarity. As our examples show, fundamentally there is a *radical* dialectic at work, by which the philosophical dialectic has been penetrated. It is the dialectic of rational control, characteristic of Western culture as dominated by the principles of Humanism. Autonomous, sovereign man should exercise this control by way of his rational thinking. This same control, equally "rationally-and-dialectically," backfires upon this free autonomy and threatens it. As a result of this, it becomes impossible to close the theoretical synthesis philosophically, and thus, dogmatically or critically, this dialectic is simply imposed upon reality, as ultimate and beyond scrutiny. Sartre's *dialectical* critique of dialectical reason shows this in a most telling way. It stands and it falls with the acceptance of the sovereignty of (historically understood) rationality.

Though born under the guidance of theory, this *fundamental* dialectic threatens the *life* of Western culture in all of its expressions. It appears both in the guise of universal practical pragmatism as well as in the guise of its weak existentialistic opponent. The latter, once more, attempts theoretically to describe how Western civilization is rooted in the notion of freedom (now understood existentially). However, it can only do so in so far as it is able to serve the goals and methods of pragmatic control for the time being.

It becomes clear, from the previous paragraphs, that, in spite of the fact that existentialistic philosophical reflection concerns all of life, its competence is confined within narrow limits. This is not a necessary consequence of the pragmatistic pursuit of control, but arises from out of its own proper place. So, what is this place?

The direction of life, together with the theoretical activity that is necessary for its disclosure, is dominated by a spiritual center. The dominating question in this center is which standpoint we shall choose from which to speak the decisive last word and to commit the first, all-decisive, act. Silence about the "last word" means that we have spoken it. Then it will resound in our actions.

In the West this word has been spoken in the language of philosophy. It made pronouncements upon the *origin* of meaning and upon man's resulting insight into the *meaning* of his existence. In so doing, it brought to light which standpoint man had chosen in order to speak (or be silent) about meaning and its origin, and to act accordingly. Throughout the development of Western culture this standpoint was reason.

We will not expand on the meaning of "reason." Philosophical interpretations of it vary. There has been theoretical reason, creative reason, perfect reason, pure reason, practical reason, historical reason, communicating reason, understanding reason, and dialectical reason. They were all distinct from, and at the same time founded in, rational, mathematical, historical, meaning-giving consciousness, in consciousness as such, in understanding, in *cogito*, *ego cogito (cogitatum)*, pre-reflexive *cogito*, etc. They all converged in the concretely individual human intellect, which was, however, declared, *in abstracto*, to be universal. The appeal for reason's concrete validity was based upon the latter, since *that* was seen as the ultimately unique means of communication.

Reason was conceived as sovereign. Since the beginning of the Humanistic idea of culture, reason was put in polemical opposition to the God of Holy Writ. As we have seen, in the course of the Humanistic view and control of life, the activity of reason in its various dialectical ways finds itself in tension with its own sovereignty and time and again has to create its own logic. Nevertheless, Western man anchors his ultimate responsibility in the sovereignty of this thinking *as* thinking.

He calls the account of his thoughts and actions "philosophy." We characterized it as the *rational* account of the *ultimate* questions. By so doing, we approximated the limits of philosophy. Here the rational claims of philosophy are disputed by other claims that cannot recognize the validity of its standards as rational and theoretical. As can be seen from what has been outlined above, this dispute can only be carried out by means of internal philosophical methods. Such a dispute is therefore called "transcenden*tal* criticism."

The inquiry as to the *positive meaning*, both of the contested philosophy and of its opponent, immediately implies a question about these very same limits. For such inquiry there is no appeal to a higher, supposedly rational court. Thus, the ultimate question, where philosophy ends and from which it starts, is the question concerning the origin of meaning, including the *meaning* of our philosophical thinking.

He who thinks that this ultimate question itself can be answered by implicating it in a dialectic should understand that such thought and action has to take its own dialectical thesis altogether seriously, and that it ultimately has no other foundation than its *faith* in its dialectical historicism. This faith itself is extremely dynamic. Moving from pole to pole, it shows that it is driven by some inherent dynamics. Hence, the question as to the *true direction* it should take appears quite urgent.

By its very nature, such dynamical faithful *acceptance* is no longer susceptible to rational proof. It can only be an acceptance of a true or false, supposedly absolute, sovereign *revelation* that is beyond summons. Therefore, the ultimate question of philosophy, which appears to be its primary question, issues in the question concerning the *revelation* of truth.

For it is this problem that sorts out the limits: Can I find an archimedean point, in which I can take position in order to decide the battle *for* the archimedean point, in a universally valid way? Is it possible to show the limits of meaning in a manner equally convincing to everybody? Can I find a responsible court, for example, Jaspers' "will" for rational communication, to which I can submit my dispute about these limits?

However, if we want to judge the competence of such a sought-after court of rational communication, on the basis of which we can decide about the ultimate questions, we are inevitably referred back to the question as to the archimedean point from which we want to decide in favor of such a court.

It appears that the acceptance of rational communication as the ultimate basis for tolerance is wholly ruled by the fundamental dialectic of autonomous rationality and rational autonomy, which has no deeper foundation and which can only have truth-validity for him who lives *a priori* out of this dialectical motive. We investigated the antinomy to which this led in Jaspers' thesis about the "unconditional" abandonment of his entire philosophy.

There is no other conclusion possible: We are faced here with the limit of all final conceptualization. It shows itself from out of theoretical thought itself. If existentialism were really serious about its theses, then it would have to make its confession about "shipwreck" on *this* point. The possibility of an "unlimited will for communication" shipwrecks in the very breakers of *real existence* itself (as Martin Heidegger indicates in *Letter on Humanism*).

Just as we do, existentialism professes that an account of the *actual* position of a thinker be given. It challenges rational and idealistic systems in much the same way in which we demand self-reflection. But if, yet, existentialism, because of its basic motive, remains entangled in the final antinomy about its limits, how much more this must be the case for the philosophies that have preceded it!

Again it cannot be emphasized too strongly that the entire argument about the bases of philosophical thought is carried out from the position of the subjective thinker (or systems designer) in the "center of operations." If it is impossible for him without antinomy to hold his ground at the limits offered exclusively to him by his own philosophy, he is faced with the burning question about what he should do from that position.

Only one answer is possible: namely the honest recognition of the fundamental position by which reflexive thought about self and world is dominated and that cannot be outflanked, not even by an unlimited will for communication, nor by an existential determinateness.

What we applied in our criticism of our philosophical opponents has to be turned back upon ourselves as well. In our transcendental criticism, seeking to bring our discussion partner to the limits of his thought, we follow the roads prescribed by the immanent structure of philosophical thinking. Yet we march by a compass that shows us the way. But even though the conclusions of transcendental criticism may be inevitable for honest and open reflection, it is *a priori* evident that without a complete surrender of the self-sufficiency of theoretical thinking, the opponent, inside and outside of ourselves, will continue to deny the reliability of

Introduction. The Limits of Philosophy

the compass. Even if we, from our side, try to analyze the state of affairs as we did above, we are threatened by the great danger that we treat the insight that we have gained as a truth for itself, which could consequently be approached as the Gegenstand of theoretical thinking, with all due consequences.[7]

For the moment, it must suffice to simply indicate this mortal danger. It is the *raison d'être* of this study. The attentive reader will already have sufficiently recognized its nature. For now it only remains to point out a misunderstanding that, in various ways, is prevalent among readers who have been theologically trained.

Provisionally we can describe the position of the Christian thinker as follows: the Christian thinker will have to submit his *thinking* so completely to God's sovereign giving of meaning that he purifies the *content* of his ultimate limiting ideas from any residue of autonomous reflection; for he wants to be fully controlled by God's proclamation and desire. Rather than starting from autonomous conceptions and rather than ascending to the limits of conceptualization by successive syntheses of thought, he will let his conceptualization entirely be *guided* by what comes to him as truth from God's side.

Here we may expect a theological objection: let it be granted that thinking ought to be subjected to the meaning given by the sovereign God, but in order to do so, I will first have to investigate that meaning exegetically, hermeneutically, or at any rate in a theologically responsible way.

Yet, if this meaning-giving will, in truth, be sovereign, it can only be understood in *faith*. This is already evident from the apostate faith *in* reason as the origin of meaning. The displacement of the limits of philosophy by *attributing* the last word of truth to it (because it transcends theoretical science) does not originate from a methodical proof of those limits, but from a *given* and blind *trust*. In this displacement, rationality accomplishes no more than logical analysis and synthesis of

---

7   This is what happens, in spite of his own intentions, to Jaspers (*Von der Wahrheit*, 1947, 743ff) and why he only regards love for (transcendent, i.e., encompassing both subject and object) Being as the solution. What is right here, is love for *God's* truth. It is false, however, to suppose that we could be approaching this love in and out of the subject-object relation. The tacitly supposed continuity of thought is a principio relativized by the continuity of the disclosure dynamics of each and every action and act as such. What is true in Jaspers' insight is that the logical "eros," the love for distinctions at work within the ethical function of the theoretical act of thought, is directed at the root of creation and thus at the unity of truth (by anticipating the meaning of faith). However, under the guidance of the humanistic-existentialistic ground-motive it misses the mark and turns away into the dialectics of existential absoluteness and rational relativity.

a given faith.[8]

If this is true for apostate faith, how much more must it be true that it can only be *faith* that opens us up to the revelation of the only Origin of meaning! But it is not blind, for He reveals Himself in order that we *know what* He desires to say. That is why faith makes distinctions, for which rationality renders its services. Rational thought can only truthfully distinguish in the wake of faith, not the other way around.

However, he who thinks that he can determine the meaning of faith and reason, and their relationship, by means of rational thought is already past the misunderstanding, even though he subsequently attributes the primacy to faith. He has subtracted himself from what is in truth sovereign.

For now we leave the deliberate battle at the limits of theoretical thought in the form of transcendental criticism behind. We will instead choose the path of a positive exposition and of transcendent criticism. In the meantime, we will be prepared to resume transcendental criticism whenever the course of our argumentation compels us to do so.

---

[8] It may seem superfluous, but this is true both for a philosophy that pretends to transcend theoretical science, as well as for a philosophy that appears to reject such pretension, while in the meantime recognizing as authority only what its own thinking holds for "pure" thinking.

2.

TRUTH AND GROUND-MOTIVE

From the outset we shall proceed cautiously, because we appreciate that traditionalism has often ensnared our thinking. It is important that we should avoid becoming entangled once again.

In Chapter One we explored the archimedean point, the ultimate steady point of reference for any thinker. We discovered that it is impossible to find an archimedean point from which we could make universally valid pronouncements about the choice of an archimedean point. We rejected this pretended universality. We reject it even when it assumes the guise of rational communication between alternative standpoints that exclude each other unconditionally. Philosophical communication is always based in an ongoing struggle between rivals who try to convince each other about absolute truth.

This absolute truth is in *nobody's possession*, and no human community may lay exclusive claim to it. That is also why it is only love alone that can be the field for such a struggle. Yet, that does not change the "archimedean" nature of the ultimate field of operation. The mutual respect that arises in this struggle will be established by ascribing a sacredness to the other's deepest conviction, and by recognizing that this conviction is none other than a conviction that concerns *the* truth.

The truth, by which we are summoned, addresses each of us in a way that is entirely unique. It is not possible to reproduce this manner of address. It shows itself in the utterly personal human face, which simply cannot be reduced to merely one of a kind. But it is clear that this entitles no one man, and *no* philosopher either, to let the truth of some personal-existential unconditionality pass as *the* truth. Such unconditionality is, after all, always correlate to the relativity of man's particular existential situation. *The* truth is in no man's control. We showed that in any attempt to gain the upper hand over it a cost is exacted with the emergence of fundamental antinomies.

Our argument here in no way denies the right of anyone to hold on to the standpoint that we oppose. We might think it fundamentally mistaken, but we grant every person the right to defend that standpoint with all means available. We, from our side, have no desire to proceed differently. The only condition we ask for is that both sides be willing to follow each other not only to what is required methodologically from the ground up, but, as we go deeper, into the investigation of the thinker's "existential" stance.

In this connection it is important to mention Heidegger's accusation of those Christians who refuse to join him in his fundamental question about why there is anything rather than nothing, supposedly on the ground that the answer has been given to them by means of information about the creation. According to Heidegger, these Christians "salvage" themselves by means of blind faith. The argument of Jaspers against "Catholicism" has the same purport.

These philosophers are reasoning here in a way that is less fundamental than we required from them. The philosopher of existence refuses to ask himself whether *his* questioning has salvaged itself by appeal to an equally fundamental faith that, he supposes, he is not obliged to account for.

The crucial point is: What are the means and the methods of such fundamental questioning? If the philosopher is of the opinion that he needs to give no account of his understanding of reason as means and method, then, in our view, he has not yet begun to ask the ultimate question.

For that matter, our investigation about those Christians who suppose that for them Heidegger's answer will suffice, will have to continue up until that point from which they begin to articulate their answer.

It is not possible to shift my responsibility for my own reception of creation as revelation to anybody else besides myself. In this respect, I am wholly alone in the midst of all my fellow humans and everything that has hitherto befallen me. I am the receiver of revelation. Hence the urgent question: *Who* am I?

Because we are utterly responsible for what we assert, it is impossible to answer this question with a rationalizing commonplace, no matter how orthodox it may sound. Yet, on the other hand, if in this pressing responsibility (in spite of all "contingency" as emphasized by modern philosophy) I meet the ground of my existence, then it will be impossible that the answer I give concerning my innermost being will not be propelled by the same motive from which these grounds are being moved. In giving an answer to the question about who I am, I cannot but give an account of that motive.

It is a *motive*, for it has made me conscious that my being in this life is essentially dynamic, and that, in this sense, it is *meaning*. And, I give an account of this motive. That is to say that I have the sense of logical distinction, which helps me in taking my responsibility. *I am to take my responsibility.* That is to say that the motive drives me and calls me to such activity that the dynamics[1] of this motive is transmitted into the whole reality of life that is concretely mine.

This motive is neither a blind drive nor a blind fate. And my sense of logic has got nothing to do with a "conscious conscience," nor with a "pre-reflexive *cogito*." In no way will this motive be fixed in the concealed scheme of the religiously absolutized "Gegenstand-relation." By the same token, it will be impossible to approach my being along the lines of the phenomenological reduction as conceived by Husserl, Scheler, or existentialism, with its dialectical constructions of "I and world" or "presence-to ...," and so on.[2]

Let us dispel the illusion that it will be easy to understand our account of the driving motive. Western culture, and especially its theoretical thinking, has been dominated by the absolutization of the theoretical Gegenstand-relation. This absolutization of the logical-analytical subject-object relation, tacitly taken for a primary given, has got into its very life-blood. To understand our account means to reckon with the complete break we seek to make with this tradition. To miss this is to misunderstand. Such a break is very difficult, since this absolutization, while being of an a priori *religious* nature, is also an unconscious one. Modern philosophy adds to its hidden status by explicitly relegating the theoretical attitude of thought to a secondary position. In this connection, it is quite remarkable that Sartre identifies the *cogito* of Humanistic philosophy with nothingness.[3] This shows clearly how the internal systematic dialectic is dominated by a foundational religious dialectic. At the same

---

1 Translator's note: The term "dynamics" may sound like it is the plural form. However, it seems to be the most precise rendering of Mekkes' "dynamiek," which is definitely a singular. It denotes the principle and structure underlying some movement(s). Ultimately what Mekkes means is the Rule of God, and the unrest indicated in Augustine's *Confessions*. I have therefore decided to treat it grammatically as a singular.

2 Translator's note: The ellipsis in this expression indicates Sartre's view of the supposed freedom and distance of the human subject from a supposedly fixed being.

3 Translator's note: cf. Johan van der Hoeven, *The Rise and Development of the Phenomenological Movement*, 52.

time, it is supposed that human reality can be saved from effective nothingness only by the penetration of the subject-object relation, disguised as pre-reflexive *cogito*, into "conscience" itself.[4]

At this point, Sartre's entire discussion of Husserl and Heidegger is dominated by his dialectical construction. Husserl and Heidegger could not admit this dialectic into the subject because they, though each in different senses, located the center of their principal point in the *transcendental* a priori.

In its philosophical discussion of transcendental criticism, the philosophy of the cosmonomic idea makes its own contribution *par excellence* via its culminating emphasis upon the primordial reality of the ground-motive. This is above all motivated by the necessity of finding the right point of contact within theoretical discussion. Though in truth and reality the primacy is on the side of the ground-motive, in theoretical discussion according to its proper rules it is merely the final goal to be reached. This follows from its transcendental nature. Before that goal is reached we do not attain to the level of communication as properly indicated by Jaspers, even though he was mistaken in seeking this communication under the ceiling of universal reason. It is this very ceiling that betrays the dialectical motive of autonomous rationality in its polar religious tension with the supposed rational autonomy transcending it. Thus, in truth, the point of contact is only to be sought above this ceiling.

A Christian philosophy should not accuse its Humanistic counterpart for the content of its ground-motives. Rather, it should take issue with the fact that they are disguised. Yet things change after transcendental criticism has run its course, when the contribution of the ground-motives to the theoretical debate in general has been clarified. Then their specific content and purpose becomes the issue. First, in transcendental criticism, the path for debate goes from the inside of the theoretical domain to its limits. Then there is the mutual account given of these limits. After this comes transcendent criticism. Then the paths will part again and lead back into their separate domains. There the results of the starting point will have to show their effect. For us, the instrument of methodical deduction and induction can only have a partial validity. And so,

---

4   Translator's note: According to Sartre, the self is immediately present as one's own reflection. That is not to say that the self appears as an object. "Oneself" refers directly to the subject. Nevertheless, there remains some distance between the subject and itself, otherwise it would not be a reflection. Therefore, Sartre speaks of the "pre-reflexive" *cogito*, which constitutes human reality as a self-conscious reality. See Ibid. 50–52.

it is already evident beforehand just how difficult the practice of Christian theorizing must be amid the established traditions.

While the motive that we oppose time and again appears to imply a dialectical polarity, we discover only one road that can transcend it. Consequently, this road *must* appear to encompass a perspective of immense proportions.

"Oh, yes, we know your dogmatical-theological compass: creation, fall, redemption, kept together by a central subjective 'regeneration.'" The initial response to reformational Christian philosophy was formulated in these terms. And this response has since been repeated again and again. Now, after all our preceding explanations, it is asking a lot from us to start the process all over again. What is even more difficult is the accusation that comes from some very orthodox circles in aid of the humanistic or semi-humanistic opponents by suggesting that the adduced Christian ground-motive is simply a reductionistic version of the overall biblical message. If this is indeed the case, then our dogmatism is beyond doubt. Then the motive driving us can be none other than the same one we are trying to combat, namely the autonomy of thought.

What then are we to do? Should we repeat our explication of the limits of "thinking," about the archimedean point, and about the presuppositions of *each* school of scientific theory? Should we again erect a transcendental criticism, and again attempt to carry a debate with theologians of various plumage? Or again, should we once more attempt to enter into a discussion with those who *a priori* make the accusation that all who do not recognize the all-encompassing authority of reason are merely engaged in "theology"? Would we not once more be cornered by some or other dictum, whether theological or not?

Let us have no illusions on this point. We need not feel obliged to repeat such attempts. Instead, we raise the preliminary question: who do *I* think that I am? From whence can I expect to find an answer to this question in spite of my own inner contradictory motives?

3.

REVELATION AND LISTENING

In the bare fact of my "being there"[1] the sense of revelation awakens within me. Whether or not I use the *term* "revelation" for this awakening does not matter. The point is this: I did not call myself into being, and the only genuine choice I have is between an autonomous investigation of the meaning of my existence and a real listening *to* this revelation. The former option would mean that I am the designer of my own revelation to myself; the latter, however, would be the annihilation of each and every aspiration for autonomy.

Over the course of human history the results accruing from humankind's own inquiries have indeed been impressive. Quite apart from what has been accomplished in other cultures, these results continue to add to the libraries of the West. And the genuine revelatory meaning of these results cannot be denied.

If revelation is in truth *not* dependent on personal volition, we can be sure that its Giver reaches humankind along all channels of human reality. He does so without any coercion to which man might appeal in order to excuse himself. The centuries of human development have provided *full* opportunity to investigate the law of life to which man is subject according to his own free design and without any restrictions.

However, there is one exception to this, and it is decisive. Yet, it is an exception that is completely intrinsic to life and hence totally free from coercion. It concerns the determination of meaning. But, here too, man is completely at liberty to raise questions and to probe speculatively beyond all meaning. This is clear from the seemingly unpunished implementation of the principle of logical continuity. It can be freely carried on until the development of a theory or a practical outworking shows itself to be a transgression of limits that are beyond human control. At that

---

1 Translator's note: This is a reference to Heidegger's "*Dasein*."

point any investigation will swing around and proceed in the opposite direction. This is to continue until time will be fulfilled.

The results of these investigations are not only impressive, they indeed have a revelatory meaning. For they are necessarily based in what has been *given*. Whatever they bring to light, even in renewed investigation of what is old and in former times has unquestionably been taken for granted, can have no other origin than that of *given* existence.

At this point, any person has to make a decision. Does he want to understand the given revelation? Today this question means: Is there a personal readiness to accept *a priori* that *meaning* must be sovereignly *given*? Will the investigator henceforth continue to choose the archimedean point for research in its relation to the Origin of all meaning? Or, does he want to uphold himself in the dialectic of positivistic hypotheses, or the reduction of existentialist phenomenology, whether it be qualified by "ambiguity" or by critical dialectic? Or, will the attempt be made to maintain a position within the practical-pragmatist struggle for historical power, devoid of any reflection, possibly under the pretext of the plurality of truth? This decision is one of personal choice: am I willing to understand revelation, and am I willing to both theoretically and practically disclose its meaning according to its own intentions, yes or no?

Its own intentions. Consequently, this means that it is not my own intentions. Especially not my intentions to leave the *last word* to my own philosophical, theological, or scientific judgment. But, the question will be asked, how will I be able to trace the proper intentions of the given revelation if I renounce the presupposition that it is I who proclaim meaning by means of phenomenological, logical-positivist, or other autonomous perception and thought? Does the created cosmos offer a "point of contact," either in its natural or in its historical reality?

This question too deserves critical attention. Indeed, what *relation* could there be between the receiver of revelation and the cosmos that is to tell him something? It seems that even the use of the word "relation" in this context can be very misleading.

Let us be very much aware of the fact that, no matter how critical we may be, from our earliest youth we have absorbed the tradition of former generations with its driving communal motive. By the Western overrating of rational thinking, we have been boxed in by theological traditions. In most cases these traditions are based in high or late Medieval scholasticism, and in a minority of cases they are based in Humanistic developments.

Revelation and Listening

Western wisdom speaks about man in no other way than in terms of his relations. Naturally, our first thought is: of course, how can it be otherwise? There is no way for man to exist except in the midst of his relations!

Yet here a complication arises. It is the priority of "reason" that makes one relation fundamental, namely the relation between rationality and the rest. It does not matter if this rationality is conceived as man partaking in the actuality of the divine self-contemplation, or as the thinking substance of Descartes, or as the concrete action of some abstracted function (Kant's *cogito*), or as—in phenomenological reduction—the origin of acts, or as contingent existence. It does not even matter if, to the contrary, the reflection on rationality is intentionally left out as a matter of principle and instead attention is paid positively and practically only to the matters at hand. In every case the basis for rational activity remains the opposition between reason itself and that which will show its position as origin in the effects of its activity.

Consequently, all relations in which man is involved are brought under the common denominator of that one relation by which man is what he is: rational. This in spite of the fact that rationality is no more than an abstraction from one of man's many living acts and actions, acquired by way of theory. The absolutization of this privileged relation is nothing but the necessary consequence from the effort, whether open or disguised, to make theoretical-methodical thought the origin of the rest, the origin of itself, and of what is thought about. It is yet *nothing more* than that.

Naturally, we can expect the following objection: it may be true that thought, which was originally practical, has tried to occupy a position of its own; and it may be true that philosophy, too, has engaged in this competition by developing its own theoretically devised techniques. Yet, this in itself implies the de-throning of Thought from its high dignity. Over against the dominant pragmatism that has annexed the practice of science, relevant actual philosophy directs our attention to the wholly unique and irreducible meaning of thinking as itself an *activity* of some sort.

This "activity" is a listening to the meaning of our existence, a hearkening that takes us into our human "essence" [*Wesen*, Heidegger, tr.]. It is an activity at the place where this meaning is being given, namely where, in the midst of a multifarious reality, we are given to understand the "whence" [*das Woher*, Heidegger, tr.]. In this understanding, "world" is opened up for us.

This is *thinking* reflection. That is to say, a reaching out thinkingly for what is "world" for us, and hence reflecting upon ourselves, in the understanding that our going out and our coming in can only be preserved in an awareness of *Being* that no longer loses itself in the obtrusive, occupying, menacing, and promising practice of life. Thinkers and poets "do" this thinking. Thus they open up the fullness and openness of man's authentic existence. If we take this to heart again, we return from the corruption of thought to its original calling, to the thinking-of-the-origin; back from modern science to the wisdom of the ancients of old, the pre-Socratics who were able to understand the voice of Being.

Yet, all in all, here too, the decision has been made concerning man's fundamental nature. While in the openly systematic and positivistic philosophies man is his autonomous thinking, be it in some degree of religious tension between thinking and autonomy, here, in the concentration on the meaning of thinking as such, man *is as* thinkingly expressing the inscrutable (read: autonomous) freedom of Being. Being as meant here is supposed to be no different from Moira, the prevailing fate of the Ancients. Its reality is shown in the "relation" between the thinking of the philosopher and what this thinking brings philosophically to speech. "The *rigor* of thinking . . . lies in the fact that speaking remains purely in the element of Being and lets the simplicity of its manifold dimensions rule" (M. Heidegger, *Letter on Humanism*, curs. by JPAM).

Allowing the simplicity of the multiple dimensions of Being to prevail requires a space between two poles, each of which is fixed by the phenomenological reduction. On the one hand, there is ek-sistence; on the other hand, there is the truth from out of which it stands (ek-sists), that is to say, the truth that is called into being by autonomous man in his thinking reflection on ek-sistence and its world.

Again we meet the original duality, brought to light by the phenomenological reduction. Apparently it is again the only point of departure for self-reflection. Again this original duality attributes the irreducible position of origin to the rational subject of the transformed Gegenstand-relation, and, as ever, it is a religiously vigorous point.

From a Christian point of view it will not suffice to attack existentialism's extreme irrationalism. Nor will it do to consider it an ally because of its call for self-reflection. Both these approaches fall short in transcendental criticism, and are out-trumped by existentialism itself. What needs to be recognized is the *permanent* component of Western apostate religion, namely, the absolutization of human "reason."

Not so long ago, God was considered an "object" of theology. Therefore, it still seems appropriate to raise the question as to whether some *relation* will yield a point of contact for understanding revelation. But, it seems that a *preference* for any one relation will always bring us, Westerners, back to that foundational relationship upon which the cultic community of the autonomous think-god is based. As members of the Western community we will continue to be subject to the obtrusion of this overpowering *a priori*. That is why its rejection is a matter of fundamental significance.

But, it may be asked, does not the term "revelation" first of all imply a relation between the one who reveals and the one to whom the revelation is made? It may not be some kind of rational subject-object relation, but possibly a relation nevertheless, and analogous in some way or other to the relations that pertain among people.

This is indeed the case. But even the mutual relations between people, which far transcend subject-object relations, presuppose and are dependent upon another basic relationship. It is precisely this relationship that has been replaced in the apostate culture of the West by the relation by which thinking man is elevated to the rank of revealer. In this way, man *as such* withdraws himself from the *real* relationship. Under the guise of its supposed closedness, man only figures within his revelatory system as autonomous and actual thinking. He is supposed to be beyond any obligation to give an account of his position as its designer. It is worth repeating that any unconditional transcendent demand to the system's designer that he drop the entire system must take into account that any so-called transcendence is itself part and parcel of the system, and thus stands and falls with it. The same is true for the "dialectical criticism" of all rational dialectic.

In this way, man withdraws himself from the basic relation because, in fact, there is no actual relation. Revealer and receiver coincide. The giver speaks about himself to himself, by means of the "world" with which he is familiar at which he dwells [Heidegger, tr.], and with the help of the dialectic that belongs to the structure of his theoretical thinking. The receiver, probably sharp in his psychological critique of those who only hear their own fear and desires when they talk about faith and revelation, is himself unable to receive. For he only dares to ask the "deepest" question (for example, Why is there something rather than nothing?) via the intervention of his "reason," whereas this ought to be preceded by an investigation as to the ground and possibilities of reason itself. Therefore, the deepest question ought to be: Why and by means of what do I ask, rather than not? This question cannot be relegated to an "understanding of Being" (*Seinsverständnis*) or to the question of Being. Such relegation does not leave the primary question behind. It remains connected with it in dialectical polar tension. This much is clear from Jasper's fundamental and insoluble dialectic between existential conviction and rational communication.

By means of this relegation, man is only willing to be receiver in hearing the voice of his own rational Being, while, at the same time, the methodically designed relation to the "world" merely figures as the instrument of this self-revelation.

As long as man himself is the Giver of such rational revelation, each relation remains cut off from all real meaning. He is *alone* in the midst of everything in which, according to his own confession, he knows himself to be *thrown*. So, let us frankly acknowledge Heidegger's honesty in his confession of the Fate of Being and ascribe it the respect it deserves. However, we refuse to trust the vehicle by which he came to this confession. No less than in Aristotle, Leibniz, and Kant, this vehicle was simply thinking thought, with the supposed reliability thereby guaranteed. *Moira* and thought, Being and Thinking call to one another like an echo calling forth an echo. All relations with and in a world are thereby construed as their mere faint reverberations.

Sartre, in his constructions based upon the self, once openly proclaimed the meaning*less*ness of life. He reached this conclusion via the same path, along which the unity of the split pre-reflexive *cogito* is foisted upon us as the last logical redoubt of safety. His more recent development serves to show in the clearest of lights his supra-theoretical asylum.

There is *no* true relation for man except the one to his Origin. This relation cannot be outflanked by thought, since thought itself, together with all other creaturely functions, originates from this fundamental relation.

Fichte at this point infers a seemingly vicious circle, and in his wake, Heidegger deems this circle to be unavoidable. From their points of view this is indeed unavoidable. For us, however, this is one more reason why the dialectic of their idea of origin is unacceptable. They have to accept a circle because "Being" (or "the absolute I" as Fichte termed it) is confessed to be the origin, while in fact it has been inserted into this position by thought itself. Hence, Being and thought dialectically continue to religiously compete for the prerogatives of this position.

In truth there is only one position possible for the reception of revelation: in the center of the circle where all sectors of the cosmos converge. Here we find the one and only root of all that exists, susceptible to no dialectical split. This root does not coincide with the origin. It is where the Origin is. It is embraced by the Origin. No human wisdom can take control of it. Only foolishness can proclaim original what it supposes to have created by thinking.

In its proper original position the Origin is the only One speaking. The proper creaturely attitude, therefore, is to listen. In its response it is free to express its listening. But this is different from the "understanding" (*vernehmen*) of late-Humanistic "reason" (*Vernunft*).[2] The latter is in no position to understand, for it needs all its attention to maintain its universal validity over against the unconditional existential demands of "Being" that it created. Thus it will always be in a dialogue, which has no chance of a successful resolution.

Listening at the place of the Origin is the most difficult thing that can be asked from a creature. No help can be expected from some thinking that would be able to "fulfill" (*vollbringen*) "the relation between Being and the essence of man" (*Bezug des Seins zum Wesen des Menschen*). Not even theo-logical thought, be it dialectical or not, can be of avail here. It too is in no position to orient the listening. Listening to the true Origin is an original listening. Which means that in *listening* the initiative to awaken consciousness is not on the side of the listener. His position is not that of a "there" (*Da*) from which it would be his proper role to "ek-sist" (ek-*sisteren*) in an enlightened and enlightening way.[3]

He is free not to listen, but he is not free not to hear the call to listen. This primary choice is his, but he is not free not to choose. And this primary choice is not about his possibilities, as all philosophy of existence would have it. Nor is it about the authenticity of existence, either positively or negatively. It is rather the choice of origin, that is to say, it is the choice for or against the *will* to live from and unto Him Who *is* the unique and exclusive Origin.

Sure, this is a conscious choice. Since it is a human choice, it involves my (non-theoretical) thinking. But it is not a rational choice. It "radically" transcends all rationality and all correlation of the rational with the irrational. That is why it cannot be juxtaposed with rational communication. Jaspers' unconditionality, together with the absolute openness

---

2 Translator's note: reference to Heidegger's etymological link between *Vernunft* and *vernehmen*.

3 Translator's note: the references in this paragraph appear to be references to Heidegger's *Letter on Humanism*.

of reason, is due to his choice *in* his radix, and is subject to the supra-rational judgment from this radix.

The point of contact for understanding the revelation of the Origin, which embraces the creature, is to be found here: in this radix, which precedes all concrete existence. It is at that point where the *first* choice is demanded from us *in concreto*. Here I hear the call, this is where I decide the central decision to listen or not to listen. This radical decision is integrally *original*. It is not a result of rational deliberation. Neither does it occur without the availability of all means at my disposal in order to make an integrally and totally responsible and accountable choice.

In the root of my subjective "being there" I hear the call of my Origin to decide between listening and not listening. That is where from my inception onwards I have been placed in the human community, together with everything else. The roads along which my choice leads me will become known to me throughout the full range of my temporal existence.

This confronts me with an immense diversity. When I am carried along by the Western tradition, trying to fathom this diversity via my thinking, in order to attain to unity in my choice, I am left bewildered. There is no convergence in all the ways towards unity that are offered to me. Contrary to what many had hoped and still hope, they diverge as much as the variety from within which I try to find my way towards unity.

Has Western wisdom therefore been mistaken? Was it nothing but a failure to point, with increasing clarity, to unity? Is it wrong that today I should be confronted with the unmistakable alternative between distraction without reflection on the one hand, and unity as existential contingency on the other? Was it wrong to abandon the closed totality systems in favor of the alternative between a plurality of axiomatic systems and the concentration upon the philosophical subject?

No. After the sober acceptance of a "discord of Being" (*Zerrissenheit des Seins*), and in reaction to all relativization, it was no mistake to re-call the point of unity, whose concreteness cannot be denied as soon as we *begin* to talk about plurality. Rather, the mistake was that it continued to allow the unconditional demand for unity to be disrupted by the principle *par excellence* of distraction, namely, the universal validity of so-called reason.

What is called "reason" is not capable of bringing forth unity. That is because, devoid of all its masks, its naked reality is nothing but the normativity of the logical function of thought. This normativity does not depend on "reason." Quite the contrary, it forces rational thought to keep within the limits of its meaning, and places it in its relative position amidst the coherence of all human functioning, where it can be used, directed, and opened up in dependence upon the human heart.

We can only attain to unity if we are fundamentally ready to completely dismiss rationality from its all-dominating position. Not only the use of theoretical reason, but the use of all reason should first of all be subjected to the "*original*" choice for or against its claims on sovereignty. Only in that way can the fundamental antithesis between rationality and the demands of unconditionality, so obvious in existentialism, be avoided. This is what is required to prepare the road that may lead to a true "listening."

4.

PHILOSOPHY AND THEOLOGY

Our philosophical opposition to every creaturely origin, especially to rational autonomy and autonomous reason, holds no less for the supremacy of any one theology than it does for foolish worldliness. Every orthodox attempt to assign a place to theology in order to direct Christian life by a combination of preaching and theory is a hopeless enterprise.

It is equally hopeless, and hence superfluous, to argue about the term "theology," burdened as it is with its centuries-old heritage. And to the extent a theology consciously includes Holy Scripture as the object of its critique, it is subject to the same criticism as the philosophies that dominate its critical orientation.

But, for a Christian, the thorny questions will arise in *orthodox* theology. We will not address its internal problems here. But what is at stake is its basic position. The first question we have to deal with concerns the *true* ground-motive by which it subjectively desires to be guided. For the tendency to combine faith and theory on the same normative level indicates the dominance of a motive that would bring about an impossible synthesis in which the primacy of faith in revelation is accommodated to a primacy ascribed to thought. We have already seen that this attempt at synthesis can only be made under the guidance of faith in reason.

By its very nature, theology finds its proper task in the area where man hears the call to "listen" and where his choice discloses which motive has been driving him. That is why theology's position is an extremely delicate one. If it wants to reflect on biblical faith, it is very difficult for theology to liberate itself from faith in reason, since it originated in a community that was saturated by the synthesis between the two. This difficulty arises from the fact that the synthesis could never have arisen from biblical faith, but only from the superimposition by the tacit trust in reason. This has resulted in its ineradicable tendency to justify itself "scientifically" when it deals with Holy Scripture's norms for faith. This is taken as its minimum requirement, only to be limited by supposedly positive pronouncements.

It is evident that this limit can be shifted endlessly and that it cannot offer anything definitive on which to hold. The double ground-motive, in some form or other, continues to hold its dialectical sway. Alternatively, the "supernatural" is connected with a rationalistic or an irrationalistic tendency in the philosophy of "nature." Scholasticism, old or late, and modern Humanism take turns. And often they go hand in hand.

This can complicate the dialectic infinitely. It also makes it impossible to polemically address all levels at the same time. Polemics will at all times have to be limited to specific conceptions. And it is important to make sure that the polemical argument is directed at the mentioned unbiblical *backgrounds*, without damaging what is positively and truly biblical. When we think of certain criticism that has been leveled against Karl Barth, this seems an appropriate warning.

Theology's difficulty is that it has a *scientific* position at the power source of *religious* dynamics. Religion's motive power originates from revelation. Just as at its first entrance in the world, the Jewish people were in the position where the creation was confronted with the Kingdom of God; in the "rational" culture of the West, theology was up-front where the Gospel was being preached. Would theology listen to the Gospel, or to. . . philosophy?

We have seen how theoretical thinking has ascribed the status of origin to itself. In connection with theology it is important to be more precise; it was philosophy that usurped this position.

Thinking is bound to its proper creaturely structure. That means that philosophy is present in all special sciences. For it is the thinker's connection with the ground of things, or his denial of it, that places him and us in the midst of *philosophy*. Whether or not a man is willing to think philosophically, his thinking begins and ends with philosophy. In our times no man and no woman, even those without any scientific training, can avoid the results of this fundamental cultural shaping force. The question is, what in his or her life will have the decisive word? The Gospel or philosophy? Human wisdom or the Word?

But why would this have to be an either-or question? The answer is that revelation and pseudo-revelation, acceptance and apostasy, are both operative at the same time. This follows from the proper "position" that has been assigned by the Sovereign of sovereigns to revelation and its acceptance.

Revelation is *power*. It is the fundamental force, the central motive, the dynamics in the root of creation. It has its own firm direction. Creation is rooted in the dynamics of this revelatory power. This rootedness is creation's embrace by its Origin.

It is an illusion to think that we can escape this force. He who thinks so, nevertheless remains in its firm grip. But he tumbles into the abyss, his face turned backwards towards the world. His life and history are then this tumble.

Western man, and everyone sharing in his culture, has to choose which force he wants to subject himself to, or rather, to which direction of force he will expose himself. From this necessity there is no escape in an appeal to being thrown into the world or to being condemned to be free.

Theology has its scientific task here, at the place of this choice. It is a choice of faith. However, theology too, is called first of all to *listen*. The question is: will it respond to this call? And will it be able to understand the nature and limits of its scientific task?

By claiming that as a theo-logical science it is the first to understand revelation, it proves *not* to listen. Instead, it then listens to the voice of apostate revelation, which reaches it by means of a philosophical tradition. This is not to say that it would not be able to rise above the level of philosophy. Rather, it is by such a claim that theology proves that it has *subjected* itself to an apostate philosophy, to the preaching of the pseudo-revelation of a pseudo-origin.

But even when it drops this claim, and really starts to listen, its calling remains a theoretical one. Thus we have to ask about its place among the sciences. This is a philosophical question that deserves philosophical attention from the theologians. Only a theology that thinks that it can attain to the truths of Scripture via theoretical thought, or that thinks that it can argue "about" God, will be of the opinion that it can employ philosophy. Such a claim then finds itself countered by apostate philosophy.

Like every other domain of life, science, too, is ruled by presuppositions that transcend it. Each expression of life, *hence* thinking as well, is bound by such presuppositions that originate from faith in revelation. A theology that truly knows itself to be bound by God's revelation, recognizes that this is true for itself as well.

Consequently, theological thought follows in the wake of the faith of the theologians. However, this is not automatic. If indeed theology desires to think *faithfully*, it will have a tough battle with the deepest traditions of Western culture, including the theological ones.

Theological thought has got itself so entangled in these traditions that it may well find it difficult to see the true state of affairs. This difficulty is aggravated by the position, according to the revelatory dynamics of creation, of the field of life to which theology has to direct its attention. The proper activity of theology is the clarification of distinctions related to the act of faith. For an orthodox Christian theology, this clarification concerns the *norms* for faith as given by Holy Scripture.

But Scripture is part and parcel of creational revelation, while faith is always creaturely faith. This has a twofold implication for theology. In the first place, it is on all sides bound by the distinctions that are studied by philosophy and the special sciences. This means that it is bound to its proper order by a coherence that is to be analyzed by philosophy. Secondly, theology, being a creaturely activity, will need to *subject* itself to the norms for faith if it is to distinguish and clarify them theoretically. The limit of theology's competence follows from the relationship that pertains between these two conditions.

Whenever theology *starts* from a duality between God and creature, either by calling "nature" the preliminary stage for "grace" (or the "area" of common grace), or by regarding it as its opposite, the divine revelation has *not* been heard. Instead, the starting point has been some rationalistic or irrationalistic autonomously invented "reason," ahead of the God of grace.

Every "conclusion by analogy," every declaration of "paradox," every pronouncement concerning what is possible or what is not possible, should be banned from theology, as long as God does not *say* so. Connections or divisions beyond those revealed are beyond its proper limits. It has no right to judge beyond what *has* been spoken by God himself. It has no competence, neither theoretically nor otherwise, in so far as its pronouncements are not an expression of an unconditional *subjection* to the sovereign One Who speaks from heaven. In short, any competence it has depends upon approaching the revelation of the Kingdom "as a child."

Theology's conceptualization is bound by (given) limiting distinctions. There is no way to close the conception around what is being received. There is no possibility of a "synthetic" insight or survey. There can only be a limited transparency, and at most a humble touching of what is given.

The only insight by which theology is stirred to truly biblical considerations is an *understanding* by faith. Yet faith, no matter how decisive and clear in its spiritual distinctions, does not yield its secret to any theory. The creation itself raises its impassable barriers to the usurpation of reason. It does so primarily to the side where God directly and in justice expects its surrender, and nothing but its surrender.

As one of the theories, theology's position is at the origin of religious dynamics. But theology's activity itself originates from these very dynamics. Within its own area of operation theology is already being moved by these dynamics. This will become apparent to the theologian by his philosophical reflection. It is demonstrated either in the acceptance of the claims of pseudo-revelatory vain wisdom, or in their rejection. Philosophically it will be the Christian demonstration of a radical rejection of each hypostatization of the theoretical Gegenstand-relation. This implies the relativization of any distinction between an ontic (read: ontological) or "noetic" approach to divine truths, as well as the rejection of both. That a Christian theology is moved by the original dynamics of God's Word is demonstrated in the joyful unconditional surrender to it, and in the consistent concentration of all "objective" expositions on the faithful subjectivity of the "theological" thinker, rather than on some abstractly-theoretical (*gegenständliche*) basic denominator, no matter how theological it may be.

This demonstration takes place in a philosophical way. For the area of theoretical practice is penetrated by the influence of the ground-motive *via* philosophical tracks. This is not so because philosophy *as* the theory of coherence could itself be the motive force. The wisdom of this world, whether or not it has the title of "scientific" or "theoretical" philosophy, can only transmit the apostate motive. As we saw before, in doing so, it functions as pseudo-revelation. All philosophy, all theology, and all theory is driven by a force of faith, arising from the root of our existence. It originates either from apostate dynamics, or from the Spirit that *calls* back and *leads* back to the Truth.

It is extremely important to understand this order of life clearly. Otherwise the spirit of apostasy will easily continue to sow unnecessary strife among Christian theorists. It is true that theology is *scientifically at the place* where man listens, but as far as the listening itself is concerned, it has no advantage over any other science, nor over any other *practice* of life. Dynamically driven in the center of his existence, man either learns to listen, or he rejects it; his thinking, which in the process can be sharpened so as to become scientific thinking, turns, after its philosophical orientation, towards *all* aspects of life. Observation, theoretical observation included, even if it is observation of faith, has to be distinguished from the act of faith itself. If the theological act of *thought* is not supported by a living faith, it cannot be considered to attribute anything significant to the distinctions of faith.

It follows that we have to reject the allegation that if our Christian philosophy is not to be viewed as theology, it at least results from a theology, and even from a bad one. This allegation is founded on the *a priori* dogma, itself of a theological nature, concerning the original duality between God's Kingdom and creation. This dogma, in its turn, is based on a philosophy that transgresses the limits of human thought. On the basis of such a pseudo-revelatory philosophy, a theology can indeed grow. But a philosophy *never grows* on the basis of theology. If that is already excluded in the case of a philosophy that wants to attribute the first word of truth to human thinking, how much more must it be excluded in the case of a philosophy that wants to be biblical. At all cost it will desire to deny the central place within creation to thinking. Only the radical revelation of God can be in creation's center. It is, in all respects, totally sovereign.[1]

Christian philosophy is at one with all those who, in their life, desire to listen to this revelation. Within the sector of theory and science, philosophy's place is in the corner near the center, since it has to give a scientific account of the relational coherence within that sector. But it will take heed not to advance to the center itself. With the others, it listens, childlike, in order then to understand its theoretical task. It would be well for the theological faculty to understand that its own scientific formulations have their base in philosophy. The route that it chooses, after its decision concerning the sovereignty of Scripture, is either humility and surrender or a distanced autonomy; a route that is marked out primarily by its philosophical traces.

Therefore, an objection against *Christian* philosophy's position as Christian philosophy requires a philosophical rather than a theological debate, that is, if it is to be a genuine debate and not just a unilateral

---

1   Theology contributes to the faith of the church by clearing up faith distinctions. This also contributes to the practice of Christian theory issuing from the church. Consequently, and in accordance with the structure of theoretical practice, it contributes primarily to the church's philosophizing. But doing so is structurally possible only if it has itself started from a philosophical basis. If faith and science are *a priori* separated, insight in this structural state of affairs becomes difficult, both for the non-Christian theorist, as well as for the theologian. The theory of the archimedean point is then identified with a theoretical (theological) position itself. That the created root-self actually puts his trust in the archimedean point of his faith will then escape notice.

dictum. It would first of all have to deal with the mutual relation between philosophy and theology. Next, such Christian philosophy would by way of transcendental criticism have to be confronted with the truth of God's revelation, which is only irrefutable for the understanding of *faith*, but which is no theological piece of work.

5.

CREATION AND PSEUDO-REVELATION

As I increasingly become aware of my "being there,"[1] the sense of revelation awakens within me. This is the sense of creation's revelation, of revelation in creation and by creation.

The question is: Why would we still use the term "creation," now that we are faced with Heidegger's scorn along with the tyranny of (neo-) positivistic pragmatism? And why is it that we continue to give prominent attention to theoretical thinking, which is, after all, merely one out of the many revelatory sectors of creaturely life? And why should we ascribe such significance to theoretical philosophy "at the center" of the sector of theoretical thinking?

The reason for this apparent one-sidedness is relatively easy to understand. Our present inquiry is not concerned with one of the practical areas of life, but obviously with the topography of all these areas. It is an overview within the workshop of theoretical reflection.

However, there is one special reason for our concentration upon this specific sector of life, which we have encountered repeatedly. It is this: from its beginnings, the Western tradition has assumed that human "reason" illuminates all of life. Throughout the centuries reason's torch has been kept burning as *the* great light that will eventually cover the earth. As philosophy, this belief advanced towards the center, and imposed itself religiously upon the cosmos as a pseudo-revelation with its perpetual dialectical tension.

Pseudos is a lie: so against what is this pseudo-revelation set forth? Is it against creation, which we identified as revelation? Obviously, this is how we have to express ourselves initially. But does that mean that this *pseudos* is capable of arguing against creation?

This is a momentous question indeed! It needs an answer, and the

---

1 Heidegger: *Dasein* [tr.]

more so, because we have also developed an argument with theology. We will have to follow the path taken by the usurper as he advanced towards the center. We did so before, in various ways in our transcendental criticism. But once engaged in a battle for the center, everything changes. In transcendental criticism both parties fight with weapons they understand and can mutually distinguish. But once the moment is reached when the dialectic of autonomy and reason becomes the issue, the party under attack at this decisive point loses all sense of distinction. This usurping party becomes blind to distinctions, because it held the mistaken opinion that the light by which it was operating originated from an independent source, supposedly to shine over all of life, from the center, throughout all sectors, and outwards toward the circumference. But, as we hope to have shown in our transcendental criticism, it appears that it is simply incapable of shedding its light over the ultimate questions. As soon as we are faced with the reality of the sovereign Origin, where the questions and answers of all parties begin and end, we are forced into a *choice* of origin. There is no refuge left to us within the capacity of autonomous reason. For its assumed competence on this point results from that choice itself.

Yet this "reason," by virtue of its religiously supposed autonomy, continues to lay claim to a universal competence for itself. This claim originates from the *subject* in its religious tension between the two poles of the dialectical ground-motive. In its historically changing circumstances, it is this subject that confesses this autonomous origin. It is in one of this subject's creaturely faculties where this supposedly autonomous originality is located, and it is this subject through which the power of its experiencing and thinking has an effect. It needs to be continually emphasized that, within the community driven by this ground-motive, a relentless attempt will emerge to solve the antinomies that arise within subjective (read: individual) thinking. That then is supposed to be the path to the future, the way towards fulfillment of philosophical thought. However, the limit of this teleology is reached when the antinomy of *the* rational autonomy of *the* human subject as such is met. The contradiction between autonomous rationality and human subjectivity appears to transcend this teleology.

In the meantime, creation's revelatory voice continues to reach its receiver. Creation remains what it *is*. That is not to say that it has a self-contained, fixed being, but that *as* revelation it remains *dynamic*. Its tendency is to be understood. Therefore, the letters and signs of this revelation cannot be self-sufficient "facts," presenting themselves, as "creational ordinances" to be studied by Christians, be it either in a natural scientific, a logical, or a cultural-theoretical way. Neither are they facts waiting to be "filled up," or to be "deciphered." Such terminology can only come from the tacit assumption that meaning must derive from an origin that can be rationally determined, and in that sense from an origin that is, in fact, a *non*-origin. There is no way for any "facts" and "states of affairs" to be *objective* but for a subjectivity that is bound to give a comprehensive account of the direction of its objectifying activity, even though this direction be repeatedly consolidated by communal means over a long period of time.

The subject cannot escape the choice of its own course of advance in the face of what has been given in its *own meaning*. The direction of this course can only be right if it is the direction of Truth. The resistance experienced in the choice of this direction, and which will not be conquered of one's own accord, is that *this* choice demands radical *self*-denial. The denial, that is, of the centuries-old consolidated self-evidence of the "*autos*" of Western culture, as the supposedly autonomous source of meaning. This denial requires the actively-passive *surrender* to the original embrace by the truly Sovereign Origin, who has been so clear about Himself.

The apostate subject will not have a bit of this. Relentlessly it will make the effort to repair the shortcomings of past periods of perennial philosophy by new rational syntheses. It chooses its course of advance, and it *speaks*. It gives its pronouncements about its understanding of creation's revelation. It speaks the first word and it speaks the last word. It makes revelations about creation's revelation. Throughout the centuries it issues *its word-revelation*. In doing so, it determines man's position in creation's time. Today man can be the pragmatic ruler, with a pluriform idea of truth at his disposal if he so desires, or he can be the residue of the once proud "*autos*," now in decline but autonomous nevertheless.

Thus the wisdom of the world reveals itself as pseudo-revelation. And this gives us a preliminary answer to our question as to how this wisdom in its advance towards the center is able to oppose creation's revelation. It does so by *speaking* from the earth, by taking the place of the Word-revelation. Thus the subject, in its aversion from its calling, determines the direction of all "objectifications" and the meaning of all "data."

Nobody, not even the Christian, will be able to rise above the divisions that result from this. Not only because of the inevitability of an archimedean point in every choice, but also because nobody can wipe the slate of centuries clean. From our very entry into the world we *find* ourselves within the particular culture of the West. This is as true for ourselves as it is for the objects in our lives. The most rudimentary thing, element, or atom of nature awaits disclosure. Even the determination of its "properties" depends on a human hypothesis, no matter how simple it may be, and no matter if it were never to be superseded. This disclosure forms part of this particular culture. From its outset there has been a conflict about the direction creational dynamics must take.

Hence, we are faced with the reality that creation does speak its own truth, but that, in doing so, it refers to the pre-condition for its understanding, namely that a word-revelation be heard. Sure, every form of revelation can be denied, but no one is able to deny that it is *man* who speaks and who acts accordingly. This is true for the most primitive as well as for the most highly developed stages of culture. The faith in "objective" reality, to be known by an equally objective thinking, cannot break loose from being believed.

The same is true for the so-called phenomenological approach, regardless of which degree of "being" may be assigned to some field of objects and their relations to the subject. As we tried to explain before, the phenomenologist who emphasizes his method (system), withdraws himself from each and every account of his own position. He assumes that as long as it is rational it is universally valid. Much can be learned from phenomenology. But its opposition to positivistic objectivism remains caught within the religious dialectic of autonomous certainty versus universal control.

6.

THE WORD: REVELATION AND THE FALL

Man cannot but express himself, and speak.[1] It can be no different for every Christian, man and woman. Our transcendental-critical argument needs no repetition at this point. We accept its consequences for ourselves. At the same time, we call to remembrance that such a condition is unavoidable. There is no other basic position.

Thus, for us the criterion for the ultimate contention is this: will man accept the Word spoken by the Giver of creation's revelation, or will he speak the first word himself? And, if he is in principle ready to receive, does this mean that he is free from the influence of the opposite motive and the community driven by it?

Yet we must still inquire into the characteristics of this Word, the Word about creation. What is its direction? And what is the direction of creation according to this Word? How, and by what means does this Word locate itself within creation? Or maybe it locates itself above, or opposite to creation? Is man called upon to let the creation speak from and unto the Word? And what does that mean for the limits of the human word? What are the outlines of the critical split between acceptance and rejection? Where and how is the battle to be fought?

These questions have been deliberately formulated from the standpoint of the *receiver* of revelation. That is, from the standpoint of the one who has to decide about either accepting or rejecting it, whether of the creation or of the Word about it. Accepting *revelation* means accepting it *as* revelation.

But if revealing is to truly reveal, as issuing from the sovereign Origin, then His Word is the *beginning*. Then creation *originates from* His speaking, and is from its very inception embraced by it. Then there is no

---

1   Translator's note: cf. Heidegger's comments on the poet Hölderlin in *Letter on Humanism*.

self-sufficiency in the creature, and no independent germinal principle. Then all its procreative power originates from the Word, from which it has its being. And since the originating Word will never be brought to a halt, creation likewise will be in a process of germination without end. Then the depths that carry creation will no longer allow for a more or less correct "interpretation." Rather, each human word will then be carried along by the Origin's dynamics. The foolishness of resistant struggle merely shows its own apostate nature as it is being carried along by such an irresistible dynamism. In short, the Word calls into being, embraces, and brings to fulfillment. There is no other source for the power of resistance.

Thus the Word about creation is the wholly unique Original dynamic, the Alpha, and hence the Omega, forever joined. Embraced by It, I desire to ask what It has to say about Itself to me.

The Word about creation is God's revelation about His revelation to those whom He calls to listen. It is designed to be accepted. That is to say, to be believed in faith, in the pregnant sense of *faith*. As such it reveals the *norm for faith*. And as such, since it is designed for acceptance, it pushes forward towards a choice in the face of this norm of acceptance. Such a choice will sweep each consequent choice along. It is the *a priori* of the whole of life, including philosophical, theological, and scientific thinking.

The nature of this revelation is totalitarian. It has an integral character. It has a center, out of which each of its separate utterings has to be understood. It is the Word of the first chapter of the Gospel of John. In an almost overpowering way it comes to us in the first chapter of Paul's letter to the Colossians.[2]

It is Jesus Christ, who, though he was in the form of God, deemed it not a thing to be grasped. He made himself of no reputation, but took upon himself the form of a servant. Being found fashioned in the likeness of a man, he humbled himself, and became obedient unto death. Hence, in his name every knee bows. This is the revelatory Word about creation.

---

2   Translator's note: (Colossians 1:15–20) "He is the image of the invisible God, the firstborn over all creation. For by him all things were created: things in heaven and on earth, visible and invisible, whether thrones or powers or rulers or authorities; all things were created by him and for him. He is before all things, and in him all things hold together. And he is the head of the body, the church; he is the beginning and the firstborn from among the dead, so that in everything he might have the supremacy. For God was pleased to have all his fullness dwell in him, and through him to reconcile to himself all things, whether things on earth or things in heaven, by making peace through his blood, shed on the cross."

Here all philosophy is silent. Likewise all theology. They can only assess the consequences for themselves from a respectful distance. They have nothing new to attribute. If the torn and spoiled secularized churches of Christianity are in Truth to be of any avail to the fearing masses, then they will once more have to listen to this Word.

It is by this Word's dynamics and its procreative power that creation is what it is. It is the dynamics of the germ of wheat that has fallen into the earth and has died. This Word drives creation on in its dynamical birth pangs. As the first fruits of its great harvest, it raises the hope for what is "not seen."

This Word is shown to us in the simple story of Genesis to which no worldly wisdom has any access. Without any regard for scientific standards of Christians raised in the midst of Hellenism and Humanism, it shows one direction: the Firstborn of all creation, the One pre-eminent in everything.

Powers and principalities are shown to their places by this Word, irrespective of whether they are the powers of *gnosis* or those of modern reason. It scorns the illusion of sovereignty for theoretical thought. It takes care of the sheep that are lost without a shepherd. This Word takes its course in the direction of dynamics, and it directs the creature according to its dynamics. It is the dynamics of the germ of wheat.

He who has made the primary choice, and answered the call to listen, is then faced with innumerable decisions. He will not be able to shake off the central motive of the culture from which he originated. Neither can he shake off the burden of the centuries from which this motive itself had arisen. His chances of doing so are even more diminished since humankind has for centuries been feeding on the cultural resources that have resulted from human cultural exploitation. When we look back over our shoulders, we discern disruption into the very foundation of things. Yet, it is as if through the past centuries we can still hear the reverberation of the voice that once said that all was very good.

The greatest mistake that the listener can make is to assume that the experience of his Christian faith is self-evidently primary to him, and that it fits the rest of his experience just like that. This is a great mistake, even though the believer may have been raised in the Christian faith since his early youth. What he does not recognize is that the culture of the West, from which he came forth, is dominated by a different motive than the Word-dynamic, and that it sweeps him along, as it did his forefathers.

However, as soon as this is recognized, we are faced by questions that, at first sight, are baffling. What is left of what was once "very good"? And just when was this "once"? In what way can anything of it be regained?

From whence comes the evidence of the apparently rotten meaninglessness of what was once perfectly good? Can I search out what came before this corruption? Where and how can I correctly assess its bitter fruit? And when I have some success in this assessment, what then is my task amid the good and evil by which I was conditioned from before my inception?

How will I fare amid this inscrutable confusion? How do I now fare, and what about when the curtain falls, when, at the end of the life-time tragedy, I will be alone with the Giver of revelation? Is it possible in some way to withdraw completely or partially from my responsibilities? Is it possible for me to facilitate the decision-making somewhat?

7.

THE DYNAMICS AND MOTIVE OF PHILOSOPHICAL REFLECTION

So far our criticism of the pragmatist standpoint of the pluriformity of truth has been immanent, tracing the presuppositions of this viewpoint to their transcendental point of orientation. The time has now come to begin a direct confrontation with this perspective in order to provide a critical answer to it and to set forth an alternative.

In practical life, as well as in the sciences, a Christian is at liberty to test and to use all the hypotheses and methods advanced by pragmatism. This liberty is exercised within the limits of an intrinsic boundary, and under a specific internal condition, namely, that he is to know the origin of meaning.

Pragmatism, with its nominalist conception of truth, claims to identify this origin in inductive-deductive thought. But, in truth, its origin lies in its thinking the idea of the relative plurality among all "axiomatic systems." In relation to this supposed possibility of relativity, this way of thinking claims a position of *absolute unity*. It is the creative thinking of the autonomous self that has closed itself off from all self-reflection.

When this mode of thinking orients itself with creative intent towards its *Gegenstände*, it will address each of these axiomatic systems in its supposed reality "in itself," without delving into their respective "essences." The investigation will then be carried through to the logical limits of the "axiomatic system" being dealt with. However, in this way, the "in itself" of the system appears to be totally different from a reality that is supposed to be independent of subjective thought. So, the "in itself" concept emerges as the methodical expression of the elimination of the very *subject* who has thought this thought in the first place.

This subject is allowed to keep its personal "attitude," or view of life. This is admitted to have its influence on the subject's choice of some one "system" of truth, as long as its use is accounted for in terms of objective pragmatic results.

So, the Christian thinker has to take notice that the "facts" that pragmatism adduces are really interpreted relations from the system used, whose ultimate ground lies in the pragmatic confession of the pluriformity of truth. Efficient immanent criticism of the field of special science at hand requires a full knowledge of this field. Yet, the assumption of objectivity should never be a ground for the omission of such criticism. Positivism and pragmatism ought to be summoned to reveal their ultimate philosophical supports.

Arbitrary thinking tries to reduce the mutually irreducible aspects of reality. But these recur within the systems under investigation in the guise of inner contradictions. These inner contradictions should be the first targets of any criticism. In this matter a particular responsibility belongs to the philosophically trained special scientist, rather than to the professional philosopher *per se*. Yet, what his special field offers to him will not be sufficient on its own. At this point the importance of the Word-revelation for reality's (creational) revelation is paramount.

"Fact" usually means a primary given that cannot be doubted by anyone in any way. However, the "fact," in order to be grasped in its most elementary meaning, is always to be perceived. This means that as soon as it is being posited, it is *eo ipso* being "interpreted." We do not have to enter into the philosophical discussion of the last century about "meaning" (*Bedeutung*) and "meaning coherence" (*Bedeutungszusammenhang*). But we should pay attention to the kind of perception that is meant here. The religious adoration of theoretical thought led to the adoration of a primary subject-object dualism, and this worship has tried to subsume this "perception" under sense and logic. But this is nothing but an absolutization. Even if joined by some *a priori* of phenomenological reduction with its "world"-correlate, this absolutization will necessarily cause us to miss the true nature of the facts.

Insight into "meaning" and "meaning coherence" does not result from some synthesis of the "subject" with its "objects," with or without some idea of order and coherence. In truth, and definitively, this insight is *only* gained by the totality of practical living experience. We will only be able to face the pretentious dogma of thought-continuity head-on, and to disclose the truly dynamical nature of all perception of facts, if we take the reality of the human act-structure and the dynamical individuality-structure of its actions and acts seriously. The intrinsic nature of this process of disclosure remains unchanged when in the act of theoretical

The Dynamics and Motive of Philosophical Reflection

thinking it directs itself towards the logical-analytical aspect of this practical experience.

It follows that the process of disclosure and its direction are to be investigated twice in the theoretical study of the facts. In the first place when the "fact" is adduced from practical experience and secondly, when it is theoretically analyzed. Hence, there is a double interpretation. Both in practice as well as in theory, the observer is basically driven by his religious ground-motive. It is the most original drive of his observation. The sifting question is whether this motive drives the investigator into the truly transcendental direction of creation, or whether it drives him, together with his "facts," into the apostate direction of the self-sufficiency of rational man as such.

What is true of this pragmatistic direction is true for all directions, including the Christian one. True, the pitfall for a Christian is a different one, but surely no less severe than the one that results from sober, logical, and "pragmatistic" positivism. The pitfall that results from positivism is a ready acceptance of the fruitful methods and results of secular science, combined with a relegation of the meaning-question to a system of nature-grace (or common vs. special grace). But the pitfall that results from the philosophy of transcendental reflection, on the other hand, results from a misleading and dangerous analogy with the Christian attitude of life.

"Transcendental reflection" is meant here in the widest possible sense. We admit that it expresses a real seriousness that is greater than thought, which sees no other task than to lose itself in the most efficient organization of the world, with some philosophical accountability here and there, the whole thing being labeled "life" and "realism."

Between pragmatism and transcendentalism we again meet the perennial dialectic of the poles of the Humanistic ground-motive. This motive, rather than being a merely theoretical matter, dominates the whole of life. That is to say that it is a religious motive. This becomes clear from the apparently definitive seizure of Western culture by the pragmatistic attitude and from the inability of existentialistic "reflection" to do anything to stop it.

The pseudo-revelational nature of pragmatism aims at the complete eradication of every idea of revelation, while existentialism's pseudo-revelation willingly and unwillingly keeps it alive, no matter how negative its answer to the question of (un-)belief may be. It even seems, when we look at the history of the last twenty-five years, that, not unlike classical metaphysics, existentialistic "reflection" could serve as the crude material for a natural theology, possibly to be used by "sacred theology" as a springboard or a doctrine. Yet, here too, the question by which the spirits are sifted needs to be asked: whither does the motive lead the one who wants to orient himself upon the compass of transcendental philosophy?

Let us merely look at the supposedly transcendental position of existence in transcendental philosophy. Existence is here taken as the focus of the religiously restless oscillation between, as it were, Being as a circle and being as an ellipse. It is presented as the ever contingent origin of a dialectical movement. For this movement it requires (dialectical) space. It gets this space either from its relation to the "world" with which it is familiar; from the "in itself" (*en soi*) over against which it is in the position to annihilate it.[1] Or it gets its space from the "object" without which it cannot reveal itself as the subjectivity that keeps the initiative. This transcendental position of existence is merely inherited from pure reason as it appeared in the guise of *actus purus*, *res cogitans*, the *cogito* of the 18th, 19th, and 20th century, the "ego" of Fichte's *Theory of Science*, the "spirit" of post-Kantian idealism, and, finally, the designer of the idea of pluriform truth in an *absolute* proclamation of relativity. In short, it inherits the subject, which since the emancipation of "rational" thought was in constant need of an "object" over against itself in order to validate this autonomous emancipation.

Today transcendental philosophy emphatically points out that its ellipse (subject-object) is in reality a circle (ek-sistence). It emphasizes that its subject-object relation is a necessary circle-ontology, rather than an antinomian ontology. Sure, this is a transcendental point of view, driven by the quest for root and origin. We sympathize and agree with this quest. But at the same time, we must declare that the desired result is beyond reach. That is because the supposed "focus," existence, depends on a philosophical and rational, that is to say theoretical, *abstraction*. For that reason, it can only function as focus if it at the same time disperses itself into its *a priori* phenomenological correlate. The synthesis of dialectical thought finds its limit where it reaches the original dualism of its religious foundation. The same is true for every "dialectical" criticism.

It may seem superfluous, but once more we should note that the decisive spiritual directions are not of a theoretical nature. It is also important to emphasize that it is not within the power of any pseudo-revelation to give a comprehensive account of the spirit by which it is propelled, nor can it account for that which is brought to *life* by that spirit. This is impos-

---

1   Translator's note: "annihilate" is a reference to Sartre's "*anéantir.*"

The Dynamics and Motive of Philosophical Reflection

sible because its structural position is within the theoretical *sector*, while the moving spirit operates from out of the (apostate) *root* in the center of life. What is being expressed *within* such philosophies is not sufficient, of itself, to make its spirit understandable. This is most of all the case with pragmatism. Philosophical accounts of its spirit are an exception anyway. The transcendental movement, on the other hand, comes forward in an almost exclusively philosophical, or at least reflective, manner. Nevertheless, here too, the driving motive far exceeds what is being "understood." It is precisely at this point that the revelation of Truth shows the decisive difference of its creative, enlightening, and critical power.

That the apostate motive tends to especially express itself by way of philosophy, results from philosophy's autonomous push forward from its proper sector to the dominating position at the center of life. Once again, the universal effect of this attempt arises from the historical domination of the cult of theory in the religion of the West. Positivistic objections that such obtrusive philosophy, by claiming to become more than philosophy, loses its validity, have little meaning for us. For the controversy merely issues from a religiously polar, hence relative, opposition. Positivism is equally guilty of transgressing the limits, no matter how sober its liturgy may be.

What we have to see now is that the same polar opposition that manifests itself *between* the two mainstreams must and indeed does show itself within each of them. Within the pragmatistic, positivistic, so-called scientifically sound direction, it shows itself in the correlative opposition between free logical control of diversity, on the one hand, and the unity of the autonomous subject in its prescription of the pluriformity of truth on the other hand. Within the supposedly supra-theoretical transcendental systems we find the same polar opposition, namely, between the isolated field of the autonomous subject, on the one hand, and the nonfree "being" on which it is phenomenologically *dependent* for its possibilities on the other hand.

In the case of pragmatism, the preaching philosopher, by the sovereign *absoluteness* of his proclamation, is necessarily at odds with the efficient freedom of relativity that his system teaches. In the case of transcendental reflection, he will have to drop the proclaimed contingent autonomy in the name of the *universal validity* of his proclamation.

In either case it is fundamentally impossible to show the bottomless nature of the religious antinomy. An attempt to do so is felt as fallacious or as a play on words. This is because decisive life-directing faith cannot refer beyond itself to anything else in time. Its actuality is ultimate. Thus, in the actuality of his faith, the Humanist gives his heart to what has taken the place of the Creator Himself. The irreconcilable dialectic of autonomy and reason, to which his faith carries him, remains hidden from him. He will try to avoid it by alternate activation of either pole (for he takes them as basically identical) despite the fact that history shows such attempts to be futile. So, he will reject the accusation of bottomlessness. In return, he will accuse the Christian of trying to avoid the unavoidable judgment of responsible reason, and that the Christian chooses a safe basis for defense and attack in a universally unverifiable faith.

This, however, is a fundamental misunderstanding. While the Humanist fails to recognize his faith, because it necessarily propels him to its assumed grounds, the Christian acknowledges it without directing himself to it. Sure, he too directs himself to the *ground to* which his faith drives him, but this is not the ground from which the dialectic of rational autonomy grows.

Again we are at the boundary between transcendent and transcendental criticism. Because of this position, and not just for *philosophical* reasons, but for the sake of this *boundary*, we will have to express ourselves more accurately. Repeatedly we have mentioned the *ground-*motive(s), which we have identified as *religious* in nature. We have discussed both the ground(s) and faith, as directing itself to those grounds. Though we expressed ourselves philosophically, it seems clear that we were on the trail of powers that dominate the whole of life and culture. Finally, dealing with God's revelation in creation, we hit a problem of menacing central significance: from whence comes this juxtaposition of the deep conviction of still apparent goodness, and the equally deep impression of total meaninglessness?

In preparing to answer this question, we avoided being sidetracked by philosophies and theologies. That would have demanded too much from us and would have made us miss our goal. Instead we followed our opponent in his direction towards the "telos" of his philosophizing, and we have attempted to show that as long as the autonomy of reason remains an *a priori* beyond discussion, it will not be possible for any *philosophia perennis* to deliver philosophy from the prison of the polar tensions that are beyond its rational dialectic. The same holds for theology, as long as it refuses to cut every tie with the element of pseudo-revelation in such philosophies.

By way of contrast, we indicated the sole main route along which we can gain a view of the exit from the tension between meaninglessness and the cultural impulse, between defeatism and the will to power, and between the depreciation of creation and the doctrine of "common grace." It is a view, but it is not a view to be gained along a theoretical route. If the view meant here appears fruitful in a theoretical discussion, and yields perspectives for sciences and humanities, then this is no more than an indication of the logical aspect of this "view."

It is important to have a clear understanding of the term "ground-motive." On the one hand, it needs to be sharply distinguished from the dynamics by which creation is driven to its fulfillment as desired by its Creator and Redeemer. That dynamics is the power of God speaking in the resurrection of His Son from the death of human fallenness. There may be many human counter-forces at work, but these, too, derive their motive power from this very same origin.

By contrast, the motive as such is subjective. It gives the human creature the impulse to choose *direction*. It can be named, it can be theoretically specified, and it can be summarized. But it cannot be grasped. Both theoretically and pre-theoretically that is impossible, since it drives man ahead in the focus of his existence. No practical or theoretical expression of this drive, apostate or not, can ever reach beyond the driving impulse from which it is initiated. Thus the motive does not arise in man after learning about conditions and possibilities, let alone after theoretical investigation. It can in no way be identified with any label of it, even though such a label needs to designate comprehensively its core.

It seems that our discussion thus far of the ground-motive of modern Humanistic philosophy as a pseudo-revelation has now been completed, whereas in dealing with the powerful dynamics of God's speaking we have indicated the *norm* for the motive by which we *ought* to be driven.

Thus, although the motive is to be distinguished from the driving dynamics, it is powerless apart from it. Hence it is subject to a norm. That brings us to the question concerning the origin of the tendencies that paralyze and halt the process of creation's disclosure.

8.

THE "COMMON GRACE" HYPOTHESIS, THE ARCHIMEDEAN POINT, AND THE ANTITHESIS

So, from whence come the tendencies that serve to paralyze the disclosure of creation? In phrasing the question about the origin of evil in this theoretical way, we are aware that we will not be able to provide an answer. Yet, this very reservation contains a positive answer. This answer makes it clear that the related question about the persistence of goodness in the world cannot be sufficiently answered in a theoretical way either. Neither philosophy nor theology is competent to provide a sufficient answer.

Take, for example, Karl Jaspers' introduction of "the en-compassing" (*das Umgreifende*) as a limiting idea. Jaspers denies that its content can be known, since there is no way to gain objective (*gegenständliche*) access to it. By this denial he engages in speculative revelation. For it is not up to the receiver of the revelation to decide how far it can go. Jaspers' objection springs from sovereign reason. It is an objection beyond its own competence. The semblance of competence arises because receiver and "giver" coincide in the assumption of autonomous reason as the origin of revelation. The danger of wanting to know is met by the danger of wanting to not-know.

Similarly the problem of human fallenness and what many refer to as "common grace" confronts us with the limits of knowing, without giving us any refuge behind the "not-knowing." Nevertheless, it is a central problem. Its central significance is that it cannot be posed or answered by itself, but that it is the question *par excellence*, which refers us to the question of God's revelation in creation. Its unique significance concerns the antithesis established by that revelation. It confronts us in a very painful way with the limits of our knowing. It forces us to look in the only possible direction allowed by the divine Word-revelation. In short, its significance is that it refers the Christian, earthly-minded as he is as created and fallen Child of Adam, to the only compass available for his way through creation. Our approach to fallenness and "common grace" is completely dependent upon our choice for or against the religious dualism of nature and supernature.

The confrontation with the limits, both of our knowing and our not-knowing, is painful. This is because Western man has learned not to want to know except within a perspective of theoretical knowledge. Its painfulness results from the limitations of this perspective; limitations, however, precisely at a point different from where he himself would design his "limiting concept."

The Christian who allows himself, with his Bible, to be thrown into confusion by the dialectics of this perspective will either capitulate completely or he will have to take his position somewhere in the synthesist scheme of nature and supernature. In either case, Christian scholarship is a contradiction in terms. This is most clearly demonstrated by the attempts, too numerous to mention, that aim to discuss the relationship between one or other science and "theology." There cannot possibly be a fruitful contribution from such "theology" to "the discussion" as long as it does not *begin* with an account of the structural limitation that *separates* its theoretical activity from the supra-theoretical presuppositions that drive it and about whose sovereign position it must nonetheless still give a theoretical account.

In thinking about the revelation of creation, conditioned as we are between knowing and not-knowing, we are to follow the only compass we have available. This compass cannot be "set" for us by some theological operation. That would shift the problem to some other compass from which we would have to take our bearings for the setting of the first compass, and so on.

It is at this point not necessary to expand on the sovereignty of God's revelation. Instead, we return to our question as to what it tells us about good and evil. We found this question to be concentrated in the question of "common grace." Naturally, this question could only be posed from a Christian perspective, since it can only arise on the basis of the integral recognition of human fallenness.

The question of "common grace" arises when the Christian takes part in the life of the world. Naturally, different attempts at *knowledge* have been made. But it is important to be clear about the motive behind the question. Our reflection is not just a matter of some sort of consideration, or of some worldview. Rather, in this reflection we are in fact driven by an effective ground-motive. We have outlined this before.

In the doctrine of "common grace" we are faced with a subtle synthesis within a synthesis. Nominally, the nature-supernature motive is rejected. In a desire to place due emphasis on creation and its structures, the nature-supernature motive is replaced by the ground-motive of creation and redemption, of conservation and salvation. But when, in an irrationalist reaction, the latter motive is in turn rejected, the supernatural is, in late-medieval fashion, conceived of as grace, and opposed to natural life. In this way, the Christian is then left with the existential dialectical choice to decide for or against the life of the supernatural.

Recently both traditions have appeared to converge in a conception that requires attention to God's presence, and even to the manifestation of His appeal, in the cultural activity of non-Christians, today and in former times. Thus, a common grace is posited, which does not presuppose restraint or conservation, but a positive action of God (in principle conceived in connection with the Mediator).[1]

If we are not mistaken, we find in this conception the influence of a modern philosophy of being. It makes an impression, because it is accompanied by a warning against non-Christian philosophies. It is concerned with their transcendent(al) depths; so much so that they are not to be considered as immanence-philosophies.[2]

This is a welcome warning. It may arise from a recognition of the impact of a pseudo-revelation, yet, only insofar as it concerns the insufficient characterization of "immanence philosophy." That is as far as our welcome goes. For the revelation of "God's presence" and "pseudo" revelation exclude each other. Thus, we find ourselves back in the middle of the problem.

As we said, the idea of "common grace" results from a synthesis within the externally rejected synthesis of nature and supernature. What is called "grace" comprises, within this idea, two concentric circles. The inner circle is the circle of particular grace. It is surrounded by the circle of "nature." The Christian principle is considered to have a legitimate place within the world. It will in the end be vindicated. Before that, however, the apostate majority and the faithful minority live out their common lives. They experience their mutual oppositions according to the evolu-

---

[1] Here Mekkes appears to be in discussion with C.A. van Peursen. Cf. *Philosophia Reformata* 24 (1959): 168. Van Peursen assumes God's presence in non-Christian thought.

[2] Van Peursen, *Philosophia Reformata* 24 (1959): 168.

tion of history on the basis of a common natural substrata, their temporal existence, conserved by "grace."

The question that remains is this: What will be emphasized? Will it be the conservation, the restraining, or the positive achievements? Yet, this is merely a question of human distinctions about relative aspects. Who would want to exclude either of these aspects? Rather, isn't the "Christian"-human *interest*, the motive from which the problem originates, decisive? If that is so, should we then not take a critical look at this interest, and return to the question of the origin of good and evil? Or, rather, to the question concerning the origins of apostasy and rigidity in the dynamics of the opening-process?

As we do so, we are again confronted with the limits of knowing and not-knowing. We can neither be safe in our knowing, nor can we hide behind our not-knowing. If we confess to the sovereignty of divine revelation, we are again directed to the "archimedean point." Let us clarify what we mean.

In our opposition to the pretensions of the pseudo-revelation of autonomous thinking, we conceived of this archimedean point as being located "in the center of the circle." That is to say, in the root of creation. In other words, in the relation that cannot be subsumed under the category of "relation." In this relation we are encompassed by the Origin, embraced by the Word, Jesus the Christ.

From this point only we gain a right perspective on the disclosure-process. And only thus will we be able to judge its positive and negative directions. For it is He who draws our faith to Him, and enables us by His Spirit to take our bearings from this point. In other words, only if the disclosure-process has already received its direction, can it be truthfully seen. We see it then as guided by faith in Jesus Christ and the direction towards the fulfillment of His Reign.

At that same moment, every autonomous pretension, every hypostatization of the creature, especially of thinking and its correlates, is cut off. For He draws our gaze towards Himself as the One who came to do the will of the Father. He was the only one with any right to speak about the possibilities of that will. And when that same will was to smite Him down, He surrendered. Here, beside Him, in that position, I am truly in the center. Only here will I be able to understand, by bowing before Word and creation's revelation. In this position I come to understand "I praise you, Father, Lord of heaven and earth, because you have hidden these things from the wise and learned, and revealed them to little children" [Luke 10:21].

This will be the one criterion for the sifting of the spirits, the competing "revelations," and the wisdoms claiming "knowledge." Only from this central point can we speak truly about the different areas of life, including the diverse areas of theoretical reflection.

At this point we have to be *a priori* and in particular watchful against any furtive attempt to separate the "natural" from the "supernatural." If we are being moved here, in our ground, by Truth, we will know how to choose in the question of nature and supernature. What we have to see is the unique-ness of this archimedean point. Truth desires to reveal itself here exclusively. Only here do we find the norm for our choice.

Conforming to this norm will *in concreto* always be "existential." Every dogmatic *account* of it is, at base, without value, if in actuality we are no longer in the grip of the ground-motive (even though its content may retain a partial value for others for some time).

As soon as we limit the meaning of the cited prayer to "simple faith" and assign a place for theology, philosophy, and theory beyond that meaning, we are actually assuming a different standpoint, and we are allowing ourselves to consort among the wise for whom *the* Truth remains hidden. From that moment on we lose sight of God's revelation.

This choice does not imply any theoretical monopoly. As will be recalled, the debate about the basic choice and its implications remains completely open, provided that we are willing to proceed to the basis of that choice, rather than trying to end the debate by some dogmatic premature pronouncement by and about some "absolutely open Reason."

There is no room for any synthetic dualism in this central point. If, yet, it seems desirable to use the expression "common grace," it is surely peremptory to be clear about the direction in which to proceed. It is only possible to speak in human terms about retention, conservation, and God's presence. But there are dangers in such human talk, which proceed both from the source from which the speech issues and from the consequences that are to be expected from the use of these terms.

What then do we know? As for the archimedean point that we just discussed, we know this point as the heart of Scripture: Jesus Christ. By dying the death of this world, He came to save the Church given to Him by the Father. Thereby He saved creation. And thus He would be reigning as King.

It has been God's sovereign desire to fulfill His history with creation in this way. For this unique desire among God's possibilities—about which no man's thoughts can meaningfully determine anything—the

Son went His way, the way of surrender. Now, all power has been given to Him and we are in no position to judge about the sovereignty with which He exercises that power. Even so, we are not left ignorant.

This is what we know from now on: the avenue of creation is the avenue of the Kingdom. Everything that does not acknowledge this Kingdom is the enemy and, hence, in God's time—now, later, or ultimately—will be removed. We know that the non-acknowledgement, the apostasy, originates from man. As far as history and prophecy tell us, this non-acknowledging man has taken life in his own hands and, as a result, by seeking to save his life, he dies while he yet lives.

In seeking to save his life he goes beyond "natural existence." He wants to expand it according to the desires and possibilities innate within him. He seeks to save it for his own purposes, even while driven by God's cultural mandate. But even so, in his desire to gain everything, he will ultimately have to yield to the encompassing architecture of the divine Architect. He yields, with various levels of readiness and with repeated attempts at resistance; his yielding is progressive and destructive, loving and hating; his hatred never opens the full hatred of hell and his love is never the ultimate surrender. He seeks to save his life, not only temporal life, but above all the life in which he "does not believe." He "does not believe in it" because in his resistance he is secretly appalled by the unquenchable flame that singes his clothes.

The issue goes to the root: God's Reign of humility, self-surrender, and life, radically opposes the sham unwholesomeness of this world. There is no possibility of a mutual arrangement, not even in the dialectical "encompassing" (Jaspers) of an original antithesis. The *antithesis* goes to the root, and cannot be reconciled. The *enemy* is *not* reconciled. He has been, and he is being, *defeated* and *rejected*.

God and evil have nothing in common; least of all some internal opposition in the Sovereign himself, no matter how reserved the speculation on this point may be. The truth is that human wisdom, which would want to subsume this antithesis under the supervision of some theological or philosophical overview, in whatever fashion, has, by that very move, taken a position over against God: He only approved of the *cross*.

Our route is between these two boundaries of knowing and notknowing. On the one hand, the opposition of the cross over against all that belongs to *this world*; on the other hand, the absolute freedom of God to deal with that fallen world in His own way. He establishes His Reign via the routes of human regeneration and human egoism, of partial capitulation and repeated revolt, of unwholesome victory and saving defeat.

This Reign *has* already come. It will continue to come. We await its arrival. Its law in this world is inevitable: he who wants to save his life will lose it; he who hates his life in this world, will find it. For Life is only revealed *through* the cross.

If this is what we do know, it cannot be possible that we would appeal to the victorious glory of Christ for some defense of *common* grace, as has been attempted from moderate sides. As far as "this world" is concerned, Christ is still being crucified every day. *This* dispensation remains bound to the horizon of the cross. The cross of the sealed and openly demonstrated promise, which after forty days became the openly preached promise. In the meantime, it is a promise. For we are saved in hope, without that hope being seen.

Yet, after the cross, something else came to man, namely the demonstration of his universal responsibility in the world and its history. It is this that seems to bring our questioning to a head.

The predicament of our discussion appears to have increased. The demands upon it rapidly multiply. The demand of constancy in the archimedean point becomes more adamant. For we can only move forward if we do *not* forget what is past. The course of history is basically the course of the Kingdom. What is still to come is based in what has taken place earlier. At the same time, what has taken place earlier receives its meaning from the Kingdom, while the whole of the historical horizon, as far as its range can be determined, can only be surveyed from the center.

Here, in this center, the religious antithesis was revealed and made public. Within the framework of the common-grace doctrine, the antithesis is also usually endorsed, albeit by a depiction of it as issuing from the human resistance against the original thesis of God's creation. That is certainly an aspect of it. But what is decisive is the side from which we suppose our insight takes in the horizon of world history. He who chooses his archimedean point, by supposing that the cross of God's Son can be included in his surveyed horizon of world history, has in doing so taken his archimedean point at some other place than at that cross. He will imagine that, in this supposed horizon, he can assign a place to creation and fall *next to* this cross. He will try to understand the antithesis in terms of creation and fall, but the value of this derived doctrine will, in practice, be as relative as that of any other doctrine subject to the dialectics of the scholastic ground-motive.

Such a position is impossible, however, for him who in his obedient original choice, knows his place to be assigned to him under the cross of the Master. For that is what matters; not what some orthodox opinion decrees about that choice. Only there does he know himself, in faith, to be at the true root of creation. Any other place is impossible for him. As little as he is able in his doctrine to discriminate the past, even so little can he determine the fulfillment of the promise. His Master is no longer in the world, but yet he is. His only choice is to follow or to flee.

If he follows and lets himself be taken along by the crisis through which the Master went, then the first thing shown to him is not some harmonious creation. Such harmony is for the prophecy of the cross to announce. History, theology, and philosophy are silent at that point. No, what he sees is a disturbance of the purpose of being by meaninglessness, a disturbance of *life* by death, of freedom by guilt. This disturbance is what the backward glance yields, and it is against this disturbance that God posited the antithesis of His Self-surrender.

This antithesis does not allow any stance for the Christian except that of his Master's way of the cross. It does not allow any evasive attempt to advance the priority of some creation "thesis," except at the cost of the archimedean point itself. It does not allow any breathing space in the continuous, hour to hour choice of direction in this "temporal" life. It does not allow any independence for what is here below, in whatever sense or degree. On the basis of this archimedean point there is no meaningful distinction between man and his "culture," or between being human and being Christian. For this point posits the fundamentally unique and integral norm: forward in the normative direction.

Thus, an investigation of man's responsibility in this world requires an account of the relation between, on the one hand, taking position in the root of creation, and, on the other hand, creation's history and architecture of disclosure.

A position in the root of creation, the center of what we called the "circle," where humankind, in the center of its history, erected the cross for the Son of God, is the radical opposite of any "immanence-standpoint."

As we already indicated, the objection has been brought forward that the term "immanence" underestimates non-Christian philosophy in its "transcendent" depth.[3] If we understand this correctly, this objection stems from the one-sided impression that the immanence meant would be merely an immanence with regard to the structure of the theoretical

---

3   Van Peursen, *Philosophia Reformata* 24 (1959) 168.

"Gegenstand-relation." However, it can be understood by now that it is precisely this structure that *dominates* the "transcendent depth" of non-Christian philosophy. So, the *first* danger threatening Christian theory is precisely that this structure, which lies at the base of the various secondary philosophical -isms, is lost to sight. We then lose ourselves, so to speak, in two levels within what is presented from the other side.

In the first place, we get lost in the attempts to cover up the mutual poles of the Gegenstand-structure. Or rather, in emphasizing the transcendent depth of non-Christian philosophy, we lose ourselves in the pole of subjectivity. The opposite pole, which gets one-sided attention in positivism, is in modern phenomenological transcendentalism merely its polar and indispensable background. In transcendental phenomenology the subject figures in a contingently temporalized shape. As such it is not merely the residue of a process of "phenomenological" reduction, but just as much of the once-vital Humanistic ideal of personality. Described as responsible and meaning-giving "existence," this subject gets all the emphasis. It is but the old *cogito* with a new name and in an expanded function (Understanding, Understanding of Being, pre-reflexive *cogito*), even though it is at most tolerated in its limited role as the subjective pole in the theoretical Gegenstand-relation.

Yet, this subjectivity conceals nothing but the abstracting philosopher. Hence, it displays the internal antinomic tension between existential contingency and universal reason, which we have repeatedly described. This polarity shows the apostate nature of reflection in its various religious forms throughout the history of "perennial philosophy."

In the existential preaching of the philosopher *behind* the philosophical system the typical *Humanistic* moment of *control* is poignantly evident. It figures *within* the system as the giving of meaning from the existential origin. It is the root of the apostate revelatory nature of this kind of philosophy.

In the second place, by skipping the transcendental critique there is the danger that we lose ourselves in a premature "transcendent" criticism of the *content* of one or another philosophy, which can easily fend off such a critique with reference to its phenomenological prolegomena.

Thus there are two ways of missing the "transcendent depth." But it would be a mistake to think that it can instead be reached by a philosophical "encounter," after which the opponent could be approached with some superior offer from the side of Christian faith. That would still bypass the apostate hypostatization of theoretical, so-called rational, thought with its inherent subject-object dualism. It seems to us that such an approach overlooks the transcendent depth of the hypostatization of theoretical thought as a pseudo-revelation. The continuing element of Western apostate religion, in its various forms, is the sovereignty of *reason*, not the contrary poles of materialism and transcendental irrationalism. It was sovereign reason that wrote the charters of that religion. There is only one source to be found in and beyond this depth: man's fall in his rebellious grasping after the Origin. Indeed, the depth of this fall has increased, or rather, it has only fully revealed itself in the rejection of the Kingdom that has come. It is precisely this rejection that presents itself in the modern pretensions of "Reason."

The Christian has to reject the positivistic tendencies to posit facts "in themselves." These are merely the correlates of the universality of logical thinking that is wholly abstracted from human subjectivity. Equally, he has to reject the correlation between the "existing" man and his "culture." Behind this dualism appears the figure we just described, this time as the historical subject-object relation, abstracted and severed from the religious root of creation. Existing man and his culture are each other's necessary *counterpoles*; they are also each other's only *pre*suppositions. As such they are indeed genuine specimens of the *immanence*-standpoint.

This "existing man" is in no way to be identified with man as created in God's image, as modern scholasticism wants us to believe. Rather, as the ground of his own "nothingness," autonomously trying to save himself from his own ruin before the face of the Sovereign, he is the very opposite. In the autonomous giving of meaning to his own "possibilities," he is the radical opposite of biblical man. His dialectically construed responsibility is a lie.

When this modern man in his conscious acceptance of the fate of his existence, in his so-called freedom to come to naught, is confronted with the Christ of Scripture, then his only response can be a question regarding the ground of *being* that Scripture teaches. But *a priori* he does not expect an answer to this question because the abyss can only reflect the echo of his own basic question.

The sovereignty of God and the attempt to correlate man and culture as assumed in this case are completely irreconcilable. This irreconcilability is based in the thesis of the ground (origin). Every attempt to graft some divine "transcendence" upon this correlation can only start from, and find its destination within, existing subjectivity. This subjectivity wants to, but cannot reach beyond its necessary and only correlation with its object. It *must* always pass by its own possibilities without ever reaching its own fullness. Its longing for being-in-freedom is only answered by absolute non-being.

By contrast, the sovereign God completely unilaterally *posits* man in his responsible position. God cannot possibly be defined by any philosophical or theological idea. He invests man with the sovereignly given structures of his creation and entrusts their disclosure to him. Man does not find these structures as dialectical poles opposed to himself. He finds them *in* himself. He is his possibilities. Not because he is continuously ahead of himself in projection *towards* those possibilities, but because his possibilities follow *him* in his fundamental choice for or against his true Origin.

Western man fell away from his Origin in his *a priori* choice for the service of sovereign reason, whatever its hues. Now he necessarily has to construe the field of his own possibilities in relation to his own groundless sovereignty, which, as groundless, is a mere nothing. Nevertheless, they remain the possibilities innate to him and are normative for his existence. He has to investigate these *norms*. This is to be done not in the perspicuity of some practical reason, but by subtracting his *faith* from the idol of having-to-be-his-own-ground, and directing it towards the Origin of Truth.

This Origin does not encounter him, as from the outside, in his "culture," calling him at the same time to take upon himself the responsibility for his "existence." Rather, He asks man to *follow* Him and thus to *let* his culture, which he *is* in this world, follow in the direction in which the Origin Himself is moving. "You *know* the way to the place where I am going" [John 14:4].

There is *no* other criterion by which our direction can be disclosed. The seed is merely to germinate. This is its dynamics. Within time this seed transcends its historical aspect, and in its root, time itself. Over against the horizontal dialectic of the inevitable choice of "possibilities" we find the vertical dynamics of normative disclosure, to be realized in the struggle of antithesis.

9.

PERSPECTIVE ON THE LIMITS OF TEMPORAL EXISTENCE

We can only begin the discussion of "disclosure" and "history" in a legitimate fashion when we take a position in the root of creation. We have to take care, however, to stray, neither into theological speculation, nor by seeking refuge in a presumed phenomenological impartiality. Either way assumes an unacceptable origin.

Ab origine, the phenomenological method eliminates the question concerning the archimedean point. Yet, it also answers it by its actual pre-disposition (*Vorhabe*) and pre-conception (*Vorgriff*) with its implied *cogito*.

As to theology, we have already seen how its methods may be the source of subtle confusion. Theological thinking wavers continuously between *serving* saving *faith* and directing that very same faith *towards self sufficient* thought. At this strategic point in the tension of the fundamental antithesis the "doing the very thing I hate" is most obvious. In spite of the best of intentions, people throughout history have got lost in the vast field of divine Word-revelation. Today, influenced by the Humanistic ideal of science, theology moves with extreme caution in its dealings with philosophical thinking, continuously paying due respect to consciousness in general (*Bewusztsein überhaupt*). At the same time, it seeks to keep itself pure with regard to the central dogma of Scripture. Yet, this very central intention is jeopardized by philosophical infiltration unrecognized in its religious sense.

What we mean is the dangerous attempt to evade the radical antithesis with respect to human accountability by appealing to those "powers" of which the apostle speaks (most pregnantly in Ephesians 6 and Colossians 1–2). On the one hand, this approach would link these powers with the structured apparatus of various kinds of competent authority in human society, especially the state with its monopoly of armed power. On the other hand, we see an attempt to save "culture" from the grip of the antithesis by suggesting that the antithesis "transcends" temporal existence.

It is true that this way of putting things emphasizes an important truth, namely our existential responsibility and guilt. We are oppressed by our responsibilities and guilt, the more so, since there is no way of escape from them. It seems, therefore, that this emphasis deserves respect, because it seeks to confront the paralysis resulting from a supposedly imposed law over against which humankind since Adam is rendered powerless anyway. It also disturbs the acceptance of a restraining (read: reasonable) "common grace," by which existence would be made bearable and hence retain an acceptable measure of legitimate desirability.

However, on balance there seems to be a trend in the other direction, namely towards irrationalism, which, as fruit of the same reason, intends to deny its rationalistic authority. So, once again, we confront the question of the meaning and direction of "history."

It would appear that the practical annihilation of Enlightenment illusions in the 20th century has definitely put an end to the Humanistic appeal to a rational "*lex aeterna*." Yet, we hope to have made clear that this is a fundamental illusion, and that the faith in rational subjectivity remains as firm as ever. Equally, the passion for the registration of the "objective" results of logicizing investigation is undiminished. But, it is true, the value and dignity, apart from rational metaphysics, of the *idea* of some supposed "*lex aeterna*" has definitely been abandoned.

Rather, instead of some supposed static order of being, to be known by rational means, and instead of natural relations, generally to be regulated by some nominalistic idea of "truth," attention has now been fixed upon concrete historical occurrence, attributed to some contingent subjectivity.

Nevertheless, this attribution fails to reach its target because, by a dialectical relation to its "objective" counter-pole, it is still conceived as temporally related either to the equally dialectically construed inter-subjective mutuality, or to the all-transcending "being," as fulfillment and supposed origin of existence (or, ek-sistence). The question of origin and attribution remains unresolved in the transcendental-dialectical relation between Being and existence, between subjective rational universality and rational autonomous contingency. In the attempt to rise above the basic position of "metaphysics," the only anchor left for man's responsibilities is the ancient idea of *moira*. The only real moment in this attempt is the declaration by decisive ek-sistence that it has understood the voice of transcendence. Listening to the *moira* of Being is seen as the only norm and meaning of history.

In our opinion, in the Christian philosophical or theological attempt to shift the antithesis in history and culture to the above-mentioned "powers," the limits of responsible human knowing are, under the influence of the philosophy of existence, again being transgressed. It is an attempt to prematurely bypass the cross, the archimedean point, which dominates the horizon of our temporal existence.

Fallen man, who out of his own accord always follows Adam, has no right, nor does he have the need, to appeal to these powers, in order to excuse himself for the division of his own heart. He himself is fallen, and that is why creation is under a curse. This is what he knows for sure, what he experiences every day, and what the Word-revelation continues to teach him incessantly. Not even the power of hell can relieve him from his proper and unique responsibility, which he can share with no one and nothing besides himself. This is his basic situation, in which no "transcendence" speaks any word to him. Rather, God Himself has come to take this responsibility upon *Himself*, as *the* Man. It was to Him, after all, that Adam referred.

His cross, though forever beyond human understanding, was the cross of man. That is why, if we try to raise the divine antithesis over against *human* defection to some "higher" sphere, we wrong the sacrifice of the Son of Man. For this reason, it is unacceptable to appeal to some transcendent depth of a superior "common grace," supposedly containing the transcendent "powers" of the defective religious ground-motives in culture and philosophy.

It seems that we have sufficiently explained how even defective culture, including its last "word" in philosophy and its apostate ground-motives, is yet bound to the revelation of Truth. In this dependence these ground-motives reveal the "principle" of the Creator's glory. But *man should not* seek the norms and the qualification of "culture" and its concrete results in some transcendent sphere that is not understood from the concrete cross of the Master. It is true that the letter to the Colossians teaches clearly that Christ has gained the victory over all the powers that exist, including those that oppose Him, but He did so *by the cross*. The battle against the remaining powers—for which we need the complete armor of Ephesians 6—is up to us; but again this is nothing other than the battle of the Gospel, in communion with the suffering of Christ.

World history is shown its destination by His cross and suffering. The course of history is determined by this center. It is up to the "disciples" left behind to announce to the world the meaning of its history, in

Creation, Revelation, and Philosophy

order that it joins with them behind Him who is no longer in the world.

In the meantime, *they* are in the world. To them He has shown *His* resurrection and victory. He has also *promised* these to them. But they themselves are not beyond what "remains" of his *cross*. *This* is what they have to take upon themselves, as they follow Him. This is the responsibility that is now upon *them* once the Master finished his work on earth. Their responsibility is amidst the world in its frightening entanglement of passion and resistance, a world that had no other choice than to open itself to the typical and individual imputation of responsibility ascribed to all humankind.

The consideration of the powers beyond flesh and blood can only incite us to arm ourselves more carefully, but it should not distract us from the human level that is proper to us. The horrors of paganism were as human and were wrought within the same human relationships as those of Bolshevism and its immediate predecessors. Yet, since the Son has taken His seat at the right hand of the Father, the responsibilities for action and resistance in human development among *men* have been sharply divided and directed. Now man is forced to accept them *consciously*.

Therefore, we cannot accept the compromise wrought by an appeal to "transcendence," however it be construed, whether it be a rationalistic or an irrationalistic theory of creation and culture. Such a compromise somehow still operates from the original duality of some subject-object relation. Such an appeal would lead us either towards some myth of "Being" or to the complex scheme of nature and supernature. In the latter case, such autonomous thought will explain "supernature" by analogy with the philosophical substrata of "nature," either in traditional or in modern scholastic fashion. *In fact* it will shift human responsibility, which, getting stuck in moralism or the contingencies of choice, becomes another mystery of the supernatural sphere.

At the same time, just as we do not accept the scheme of nature and supernature, we also reject every thought of some sphere that supposedly "transcends" the creation as it is known to us. There are creatures and creational relations beyond our ken. But they are, as such, no more hidden than those with which we have to deal within the so-called normal horizon of life. They are equally *created*.

The scheme we reject stems merely from the desire of human "reason" for autonomy, no matter whether this "reason" is specified as rational or as existential. If it is true that creation *only exists* in its being encompassed and carried by the divine Origin, then it is this Origin that from moment to moment effectuates and reveals itself within the creature. Then man has no other calling but to be a willing instrument of revelation. God reveals Himself *through* man and He reveals the creation, in which he has his place and which is dependent on him, *to* man.

Within this revelation, the creation, concentrated in the Firstborn of all creatures, appears as the germ of the *coming* Kingdom, which has now come. Only with this future in view can creation with all its structures and its history be understood. The history of creation is the development of the creaturely seed. This is the unfathomable mystery of the dying corn of wheat. Three times the voice from heaven spoke unto the Firstborn prepared for sacrifice. At the third time, Heaven sealed the prophecy of the corn of wheat. "These things I have spoken unto you in proverbs" [John 16:25, KJV]. The death of creation in its Firstborn speaks no longer in proverbs, but plainly of the Father: ". . . because the prince of this world now stands condemned" [John 16:11].

The history of creation. But what about the meaning of world history? From whence and with what perspective can it be surveyed? What do philosophy and the discipline of history have to say on this point?

10.

HISTORY AND THE DYNAMICS OF DISCLOSURE

Philosophy and the science or discipline of history can teach us very little about the meaning of world-history. As we have seen, every attempt to transcend this limitation claims revelatory significance. Confined to the theoretical sector of life, philosophy and, in its turn, the science of history, can only teach us anything at all if they proceed *from* revelation. This is, in fact, what they do.

They either speak from the revelation of Truth or they make their pronouncements from some pseudo-revelation. In the West they speak from the pseudo-revelation of autonomous reason in all of its subsequent dialectical phases of development.

As we have seen, when either a naïve logicistic or a "critical" positivistic view of history takes the historical "facts" for what happened in "history," then it speaks from a standpoint of pseudo-revelation. This is the pseudo-revelation of faith in abstract theoretical thought as the autonomous origin of reality. It is supposed to be beyond critical inquiry.

Positivistic historical theory followed in the wake of idealistic historicism, while rejecting the latter's transcendental motive. The history of the nineteenth century, declining in its positivism, has not been able to regain this transcendental motive, since it was the Humanistic ideal of personality that was dying. Under Schleiermacher's influence, Dilthey's retreat to the subject got stuck in a defeatism, without any direction or resistance.

Then phenomenology, influenced by this retreat into the subject, turned against positivism, but by using parts of its method all the same. It paved the way for a new, initially contingently-individualistic, historicism. By now it has become quite complicated and is still developing apace. The so-called critique of dialectical reason, attempting to take the place of Dilthey's critique of historical reason, seems to replace all "value judgments," as well as Dilthey's "Humanistic" methodologies, with the categories of existentialistic phenomenology. It seeks, however, to re-engage the inner agent of history, which was rejected by both Dilthey and Heidegger.

This is an inversion of the dialectical religious poles. In the beginning of the 20th century this inner agent disappeared. It was sacrificed to the defeatist idea of freedom. Now it reappears from the Marxist ideal of control. Just like Dilthey's "critique" attempted to safeguard freedom for theoretical activity, the existentialistic categories merely aim to call for a principle of freedom over against the continuity of pragmatism. In either case, this is of no avail, because both "critiques" are unable to fathom the character of the practical-religious transgression of historical-theoretical activity in the fundamental dialectic at hand. They are unable to do so, since science and philosophy have merely a limited competence, while the Humanistic philosopher *cannot* recognize that limitation *ex origine*.

A philosophy of creational revelation must reject both positivism and historicism. It is not necessary to warn once more against the attempt to introduce historicism into some supra-natural realm, according to the fashion of a late idealism. We have sufficiently opposed such danger from a modern synthesist motive. Equally, our rejection of the positivistic attitude of thought, when we dealt with the meaning of the "facts," seems sufficient. As concerns the positivistic attitude of thought, we find the most grotesque mentality in those Christian historians who suppose that they are capable of proceeding in an "exact scientific" manner, maintaining the crux of "causality," while continuing to believe in some, necessarily inscrutable, meaning of history.

Naturally, any decision about the questions raised here, is of a *philosophical* nature. A philosophy of human action in the broad sense has to reckon with the influence of the *inner* act life of man. It seems appropriate to spend a few words on the philosophy of the cosmonomic idea, for in dealing with man's inner act life, it is at the center stage of its operations.

We have become accustomed to hear about the philosophy of the cosmonomic idea as a "system." There is a preference to depict it as "static." It is portrayed as closely allied to some critical ontology emerging in the transition from neo-Kantianism to phenomenology. It is even portrayed as a scholastic, intellectualistic system, attempting to survey every fault, and to fathom every mystery.

Such qualifications are attempts to attack it where it is supposed to be vulnerable. Yet, the impulse for such attacks has a deep origin. It is true, the philosophy of the cosmonomic idea was only able to theorize in its "time" by the means available to the communal thought of its era. But neither in its own explanations nor in its position over against "perennial" (!?) philosophy was it static in its conceptions. By no means! That is why it also has relevance for the periods following its inception.

The main thrust of its attack was against the age-old deadly paralysis of science and philosophy that resulted from the divinization of theoretical thought itself. It was aimed at the metaphysical hypostasis of the theoretical "Gegenstand" relation, which arose before this term could be invented, and which remained firmly established in the heart of philosophy even after the term was despised. The philosophy of the cosmonomic idea discovered the hidden religious dialectic, which was antinomic in itself, that was operating *in cognito* underneath this paralysis. It opposed this paralysis by its thesis of *disclosure*, a dynamic principle that broke through the continuity of supposedly autonomous thought and directed attention to the original and divine status of the *structures* of modality and individuality. This was the reason for the religious opposition by which it was met.

In reality, the principle of disclosure is not secondary with regard to the modalities, as if the latter could be subsequently related to each other in some dynamic relation. The modal aspects express the dynamics of creaturely meaning. The *dynamics* is primary. It drives and it moves on. But, in his opposition, man continues to maintain himself in his idols. The silent, most powerful idol of Western "culture" is the illusion of thought-autonomy. This idol does not tolerate any dynamics beyond its grasp. It opposes it by some dynamic invention of its own that, like every idol, misleads by its ability to ensnare.

Disclosure, along with its defective paralyzing apostate counterforce, is driven from the religious center of creation, under the impulse of fundamental communal motives of a religious, integral nature. We repeat, it is possible to deal theoretically with these motives, but again, this dealing is necessarily guided and driven by some such integral driving force: the motive is itself a moving *force*.

In his *acting* man lives in community with humankind and with nature. The direction of disclosure takes concrete shape in this acting. Its dynamics originate from the root of creation, and should only be directed toward creation's fulfillment. That is why this dynamics primarily appeals to man's faith. For man cannot search for the Origin of creational revelation but by faith. This is his freedom by which he is driven beyond the multifacetedness of creational meaning, in order to understand that very meaning and the One Himself, from Whom that meaning orginates.

For this is precisely the miracle of creational revelation: It drives us beyond towards the *Word* that has been spoken within it and about it. This Word made flesh bowed obediently under its structures, in order that these structures would join in with it. Thus, He would lead them towards their destination. There is no other destination for creation, as we have seen.

Even in his defection, man cannot liberate himself from this law and structure of disclosure. According to the order beyond his choosing, it is by the law of faith that he makes the rich diversity of life decay into an idol. In the Western cult of theoretical thought, man, in his faith, has subjected life to the direction that proceeds from theory. And, as in every cult, acts and actions, which retain their own specific meaning, were used for its service. The acts of thought were installed in the service of this faith-cult of reason. Under the guidance of faith in supposedly autonomous thought, the direction of their dynamics was turned towards the glorified idol. Yet, the analytical modality of the act of thought has its proper (logical) subject-object relation. But in the apostate cult of faith this relation is abstracted from its structural and modal coherence, elevated to the altar and declared to be the dialectical foundation of reality. Western science and philosophy have pre-consciously, consciously, and post-consciously, embroidered this allegedly incontrovertible pattern.

There could be no greater misunderstanding than the attempt to explain our thesis in terms of the background we have just described. It is only possible to *contest* the hypostatization of the logical subject-object relation when guided by *that* faith that follows the *vertical* direction of disclosure, even in the (theoretical) act of thought.

The idol of sovereign "reason" can only validate itself under the continuous tension between sovereignty and reason; but they mutually suppose and cancel each other. As we saw in our introduction, the religious nature of this hypostasis shows itself in its inner polar tension in the practice of Western cultural history. It has an impact far beyond the philosophical cult, which is, after all, mostly forgotten nowadays.

By contrast, the confession of the vertical and endless dynamics of creation has a far-reaching and decisive significance for philosophical insight regarding the meaning of history, and, connected with it, the demarcation and the task of the science of history itself. The vertical-dynamic structure of creation can never be reconciled with the cyclic, progressive, or dialectical hypotheses of either the mythologizing or the scientific view of history. Its dynamics makes any halt in time impossible.

Both progression as well as "return" are inherent in the historical *aspect* of creation. Yet we cannot retain them in their usual meaning. Since we have seen how Humanism's dialectic is refracted into the practice of historical science, it seems that we no longer have to be concerned with its dialectical historical views. Each of these views is conceived in the horizontal plane of history. Their conception urges the thinker to choose a point *for himself* within the real *course* of history. At the same time, this point is necessarily taken up into history's flow. Ultimately it cannot but show itself in the inner contradiction of control-at-rest in conceiving and judging, on the one hand, and progressive movement (teleology, "return") on the other hand. For rest and movement mutually presuppose each other.

The thinker, taken up in the movement of history, as he himself declares, reaches in faith beyond the consequences of his own conception, in order to make his own judgment of history plausible. In doing so, the existentialistic "presence to . . ." must ultimately, even dialectically, "split" consciousness itself.

This antinomy does not present itself for Christian philosophy, since it recognizes that it is not possible for the vertical structure of human activity to be closed off in time. It does not agree that man is wholly *swallowed* by any flow of history. Hence, man does not have to withdraw dialectically from it in order to obtain a judgment about it. For history is the history *of* man. It is the history that *he* makes. Therefore, his living through it cannot but be a consequence of his action.

That man has his place in history means that in each of his actions he is *also* historical. A "historical" description of man's actions must begin from this historical "aspect." But such a description requires a comprehensive treatment. Historical meaning cannot be understood apart from its coherence with the meaning of all other aspects. For history means *disclosure*. "Historical" occurrence is investigated in order to know *what* occurs. That is different and more than occurring as such, and only in coherence with this does "historical occurrence" have its meaning.

This self-expression of *what* occurs *within* historical meaning was dubbed the "historical aspect" by the philosophy of the cosmonomic idea. Rather than ultimate power*lessness*—the "freedom" of post-positivistic historicism—it left no doubt that this aspect evidences man's formative *power*, in the sense of the *responsible* exercise of power.

In this responsible creational power-formation we meet the true meaning of human freedom. It had to be repeatedly discovered by historicism. But its meaning could never be understood. Such understanding was barred by historicism's *a priori*. Just like its positivistic counter pole, it *bounded* every judgment within the duality of the theoretical "Gegenstand" relation, which it religiously supposed to be original. By the hypostatization of logical-analytical meaning, all -isms, hence historicism as well, function as basic denominators of a secondary-dialectical nature.

Existentialism's portrayal of this *bondage* as *the* antinomy of our *existence* is nothing but an attempt to escape from the basic antinomy of the bondage of the Humanistic religious choice of position. For this latter bondage is nothing but the *a priori* attribution, *at all cost*, of philosophical *thinking* as sovereign, the ultimate revelation. To say it again: it is an attribution that is paid *at all cost*: The antinomy of a contingently-free acceptance versus an apodictic universality is ignored.

We can only understand human freedom in history if we release our understanding from the age-old bondage to the abstract duality of a supposedly sovereign theoretical thought. It is an idolatrous, god-like bondage. Its dissolution can only occur beyond its sure reign. Freedom can only be wrung from its grip in an all-decisive battle. This again brings us to the extreme limits of transcendental criticism. Here again we fundamentally and antithetically set the unavoidable dynamics of disclosure over against each and every horizontal understanding of history.

Man's resistance against his creaturely destination causes him to take this disclosure as bondage. Yet, at all cost he will deny such coercion. Its admission would imply his religious capitulation. Rather, he will try to engage the dynamics in his own service, in the cult of his many idols, each of which represents human sovereignty. According to its inner law, this dynamics occurs throughout the generations of a common culture, and through the successive tensions of its religious dialectic. Therefore, it is not possible for man to gain a direct insight into it. Nor is it possible to directly change its concrete course.

And man in his defection has no practical need to do so. Seeking himself only, he realizes himself within his (concrete) "possibilities." These present themselves to him in situations that vary in scale. They yield a wide perspective for so-called "shapers of history" and encompass the "situations" of many smaller minds. It is existentialism's endeavor to point out the mutual coherence between these various responsibilities. Yet this coherence remains enclosed within the horizon of the "critique of dialectical reason," and is consequently, by a "rational" critique, safeguarded against any deeper insight.

The law of disclosure provides the Christian with a simple parole:

"You, follow *Me*." This command leaves an integral survey of the course of "historical development" beyond his reach as well. It confines his view to the intrinsic process of disclosure in so far as it takes place within the scope and time-span of his life's calling within his community. For the Christian *theory* of history, the only question is what humankind, within the period studied, have done within and with this process. Possibly some "effects" will be found here or there. These will necessarily be limited to their modal-historical meaning. In the meantime, the "facts" that he investigates according to their historical modality will be most variously qualified. This is to say that time and again, the *direction* of disclosure will have to determine his judgment. Limited within smaller or larger perspectives, his discoveries will never provide him with a grasp of God's guidance, nor even of His "times and opportunities."

Christians' decisions concerning their organizational and organizing action in the world is also only determined by this single and simple parole. It will not grant them the hope for the liberation of temporal life. Such liberation only comes as the radical redemption of creation and is not entrusted to human hands. Christians know that they and the whole (Christian) cultural enterprise, together with the whole of humanity, are subject to the decay that results from the reversal of the process of disclosure. And they know that the Creator has put disclosure in the hands of the Firstborn. He spoke: "What I mean, brothers, is that the time is short . . . those who use the things of this world [should live] as if not engrossed in them" [1 Corinthians 7:29, 31]. This word puts them on the crossroads of creational revelation. There they are confronted from all sides by the onrushing question: You, Christians too, what are you doing here?

This question hits us in the face. When we have felt the need to formulate it, it strikes us even more. As we said, philosophy and historical science are only of limited relevance in dealing with it. The history we are thinking about is the history of *humankind*. Without enlarging this answer, but yet formulating it more completely, we can say that it is the history of *creation*. In the first place, therefore, it is not the history of individual people, races, or cultures. Nor can the "totalization" of these individuals be expected from critical dialectical reason. Its "horizontal" claims appeared to be at odds with the vertical dynamics of given creatureliness.

It is the history of "humankind," we said. This raises some difficulties, especially in the face of modern claims at "totalization." The questions concerning the unity of humankind and interhuman connections were crucial in phenomenological thought. Yet these problems cannot be solved either by biological universalism, as in the idea of a creation "from one blood," nor by classical idealistic Humanism, nor by any form of individualism, and not even by the dialectical technique of the "interiorization of the exterior,"[1] understood as an actual act. The fundamental meaning of the transcendental question that needs to be asked here does not allow of any philosophical answer. Here too, we need to break up the common denominator of the subject-object relation. If it is taken as an ultimate given, beyond critical examination, we are left without perspective. And the basic transcendental question at issue here is the more urgent since we repeatedly acknowledged that it involves an individual choice of position.

Let us look briefly at Sartre's discussion with Heidegger in *Being and Nothingness*. Where Heidegger teaches a theory of "being-with" (*Mitsein*), Sartre wants to maintain the most absolute individualism without falling into solipsism. Sartre's reproach against Heidegger is that the latter's conception of "being-with" as an ontological structure approaches abstract Kantianism. But abstract Kantianism cannot explain any concrete "being-with." Under the pressure of the in-itself, Sartre made existence retreat into nothingness. Hence, he has no other possibility but to construe sociality from the subject-object dialectic in a contradictory-logicizing fashion. Heidegger, on the other hand, bases all individual existence in Being, the mere Transcendence as such (*das Transzendens schlechthin*).

Sartre, therefore, has no choice but to posit all concrete relations from his own, isolated archimedean point, namely, the "for-itself" (*pour-soi*) as the foundation of man's own nothingness. From this archimedean point his reproach of Heidegger is correct. But Heidegger will reject it by saying that it is not up to existence to judge about the unity or non-unity of being and non-being in Being. All it can do is exist in its world, listening to the voice of Being. It bears strictly its own responsibility, arising from the purely personal Appeal to exist authentically.

With respect to the latter, Sartre says: "To posit the problem [of inter-human relations] on the level of the incommunicability of individual subject was to commit a *proteron husteron*, to stand the world on its head" (*Being and Nothingness*, 246). For it would yet be against the background of original collectivity that authentic existence would have its place. On this point Sartre has not understood Heidegger, for Heidegger is serious in his strict use of the term "authenticity." Human existence in authentic-

---

[1] Translator's note: Sartre, *Being and Nothingness*.

ity cannot be understood from some inauthentic "being-with." Rather, all forms of inauthenticity derive their meaning from the background of authentic existence.

From his archimedean point, namely historical existence as existential residue of phenomenological reduction, Heidegger came to the idea of fullness of meaning beyond the primary subject-object duality, in order from there to sanction the peculiar nature of his archimedean point. Sartre holds on to the irrational *logical* subject-object dualism. On this "plane" there is no room for Heidegger's appeal to all men to thinking-of *Being* (see Heidegger's reproaches against Sartre in *Letter on Humanism*).

We see again how the various parties are beyond the possibility of understanding each other, due to the shifts in the tension of the fundamental religious dialectic. While Heidegger's philosophy of existence is more and more being charged from the pole of human *sovereignty* as such (be it in defense against it), Sartre attempts to save the same sovereignty by means of dialectical-logical *control*. Again, one will search in vain for a theoretical solution to these unavoidable antinomies. We would be left tossed to and fro between solipsism and (either dogmatic or critical dialectical) totalitarianism.

As always, these antinomies carry us towards the limits of thinking. They show how the answer to the questions that are structurally transcendent to thinking has been given from beyond these limits, both *qua* direction and in principle. We can only start on a *new* road if we dare to engage the usurper beyond the limits of thinking with a counter-*confession*.

The second point concerns history as *history of humankind*. It is only possible to understand human history, inclusive of its inherent forms of community in their development, from the *true* revelation. As such this history is more than human history.

This does not simplify the understanding of history as the occurring history of creation. For if we abandon autonomous reason, we see ourselves completely *engaged*, not in the dialectic of that reason, but in the process of creation's *disclosure*. Because of this engagement, apart from what has been *revealed* about it, any conclusion concerning the temporal beginning or end of history is beyond us. Equally, this engagement makes it impossible for us to apply a fixed criterion for the concrete forms of man's developing social life. The same is true for human activity, since its individual qualification is determined by social structures. Thus we get to the point, already hinted at, where common task and personal responsibility meet. Here the question of the way of the cross once more becomes truly relevant.

At this point there is no room for ethics in the usual sense. Such is merely the result of the hypostatization of the rational or existential *nous praktikos*, even in its most modern guise. Man is called to action from the task given to *humanity*, in its societal differentiation. This call directs him to the given natural sides of creation. There he finds the primary objects for disclosure.

By acting in community, man has to gain insight into what is historically and creationally given. Thus he gains an insight for action. On the basis of this insight he has to act, molding history. What is the disclosing stimulus for his disclosing formative action? That is the decisive question. The decision comes from the archimedean point that he chooses for his insight, rather than from some understanding of "practical reason."

Again, it is the archimedean point that is decisive. We discussed its meaning in Chapter Two. First we dealt with its meaning for philosophical reflection. It appeared that the choice for some archimedean point is irreducible and beyond the control of "reason." For, as we saw, any appeal to reason implies such a choice. It also appeared that the explicit or implicit idea of the origin determining all meaning, and hence the content and purport of each and every philosophy, is completely and one-sidedly dependent on such choice.

Secondly, we dealt with choosing *in concreto* and the norm for it. Here too, we could only speak from our own archimedean point. Just as we asked for a fair account of the *a priori* choice of our partner in dialogue, we gave one ourselves. We submitted to being invited to choose our position in the true root of creation as the norm for our choice. Thus showing that we join in at the base of the cross of the Rejected One, by Whom the world was made and by Whom God will judge the world. But we were very emphatic: it is at the base of His *cross*, where we, lost as we are, are directed forward in history. When we discussed antithesis and common grace, we reiterated the necessity of this original choice.

Again, this is to say that we are here concerned with a confession of the philosopher, in itself neither philosophical nor theological, but strictly pre-theoretical. This confession lays bare the basis that is demanded by the structure of his life, and that is *consequently* the basis for his philosophizing as well. This is the same, for example, with the one who bases himself on the *a priori* acceptance of "reason," be it with the addition that reason has such a prerogative only in matters of theory. Nevertheless, not by way of proof, but by way of confession, the last word is universally attributed to reason.

It follows that the archimedean point is not a starting-point for deduction, since starting-points are governed *from* the archimedean point. They are seen and judged *from it*.

We now have to deal with two questions of great importance if a faithful insight into the meaning of history is to come into view. The first question is this: If personal responsibility is decisive within the human community, and cannot be shifted onto the community, and if, nevertheless, man is only man within this community, then what does it mean to choose one's archimedean point in the root of creation? The second question is this: If at all times man is, together with all and everything, *taken up* in the process of disclosure, how, then, can he gain an insight from an archimedean point into the formative action that is required from him?

On the standpoint of static rationalism, as well as on the standpoint of the dialectical shifting of the ephemeral subjectivities of Sartre's dialectical reason, both questions remain unanswered.

It was already clear that reflective thinking about and dealing with the archimedean point occur from this very point itself. This was the reason for the antinomy of the universality of the existentialist's utterances from his "existential" archimedean point. The choice of position as such cannot be the point of censure. Rather, it was the silent *a priori* claim of philosophical universality, and its subsequent assumption of exclusivity in *rational* communication. We, from our archimedean point, opposed this claim by requiring the transcendental-critical dialogue.

Man's reflection is from beginning to end stirred in his acting, including his inner acts. This acting—in which he lives and experiences himself—is not an acting *in relation to* some "world." We rejected all original dualism. Hence we are under no obligation to prove some relation, nor some concentration. If we still want to make a distinction between acting and inner acts, it is merely to pay attention to the activity that is confined within the individual person, which is, in principle, out of sight to others. As well, the content of that activity is only possible by man's all-sided coherence within humanity with its objects.

Man *has to* act. This has been so within the process of disclosure since the beginning of creation. As such, without having asked for it, man is an instrument of revelation. The creation is revealed *through* him. That is to say, through him creation's Maker, man's Maker, reveals Himself. The issue is what He has to say along this road, what He has to say to *all* men.

This eliminates every mysticism or "projection" of a supposedly independent "inner" life, in which man would be isolated and intimate with himself, with the dust of the earth, and with God, apart from his commerce within the "world." God's way with man is through his Word, *in Christ*. His way of the cross travels *through* creation, which is to be saved, and which He bore and bears in Himself, in His dying and rising. As the Master, so the disciples. "Sell everything you have and give to the poor, and you will have treasure in heaven" [Luke 18:22] was meant in relation to creation. Only thus can it have its meaning. It may even mean that we have to "sell" our inner pietism as one of the creational goods to be relinquished. The disciple may be invited to rest a while, but he is not allowed to sojourn: "you will not finish going through the cities of Israel before the Son of Man comes" [Matthew 10:23].

What God has to say can be heard in one place only. If all are called to that place, I will find *humankind* there *and* myself as its member, with my personal responsibility for it. Only from there does humankind form one community, *the*—real—community, and only from this place can its various communities be explained. It is necessary to pay attention to the various responsibil*ities* of the various "members." But we should not put all emphasis there. In doing so, we would lose the center until we dialectically reached the "world" pole, as something in itself, from which we could erect a new cult. What is important is that we stick to the *Head*. In that way I am personally a revelational instrument, and thus an instrument for the conservation of the body, i.e., humankind. Only in its Head does creational revelation reveal its meaning. When I look at Him, I again know myself within creation only on the road of the cross. What do I do, as personally responsible for humankind, the same humankind that prepared my birth, and put me in a world that was what it was when I arrived?

What does it mean that I am from my very birth taken up in the process of creation's disclosure, while I am yet being called to take my stance in the only archimedean point in order to take up my own responsibility? Historicism demanded the choice of a *fixed* point, which, by its own observations, it regards as taken up in the movement that denies all fixation. Does not the demand for an archimedean choice in the midst of the process of disclosure come very close to this antinomy of historicism? It may seem so.

For, in the first place, we cannot say that our archimedean point is in concreto beyond the progression of historical time. The cross once stood on this earth, but we do not accept a relic of it. Nor has the place of the grave, which was opened from heaven, been marked. Secondly, it was for many centuries before the cross and resurrection that humankind was actively seeking its way. It found death in its search for life, it tilled the earth in order to eat its bread in anguish and to meet its lust, and it left behind the trails of what appeared possible, as well as the ruins of its failures. Once the "times of innocence" were over and personal responsibility was no longer avoidable, while at the same time the sources of cultures sprang wide open, it did not change its course. "If the world hates you, keep in mind that it hated me first" [John 15:18]. What has been disclosed by the process of disclosure? Here the question of the archimedean choice becomes very critical, and all problems connected with it return.

In two ways the dynamics of disclosure is normative. In the first place, it is normative in its determination of meaning, a determination that is independent of man's will. Man, in choosing himself, follows the disclosure just as far as it satisfies his choice of self. On any other point he resists and closes off. This closing off, too, has its archimedean point. The Son remains in the house forever. The slave opposes the Son. Hence the meaning of disclosure is pregnant in the call to bow before the Son. With Him we have to deal, and with Him alone. That is why our archimedean point has got nothing in common with the antinomies of historicism. We live with Him Who lives. He is alive as the concrete root of creation, here and now. We know Him by His Spirit, *because* He knows us.

This is strictly personal. What every man does on and with the ruins of creation is a strictly personal responsibility. Blown by the Spirit, in the middle of his concrete earthly existence, he *stands* in the true archimedean point, taking heed lest he fall. Always being coerced to act, he holds on to this anchor place . . . in order to be *free*. From this point he studies the reactions to his own and others' actions, taking into account the perspective of the generations, in order to fathom the meaning of the creational structures.

In doing so, he has no desire for an epistemological theory in the usual sense. Every such theory is based in the *a priori* of the autonomy of reason with its hypostatization of the traditional duality of subject and object. This is not to say that he is not interested in the world's endeavors at theory and science. If he is well acquainted with its methods and its historical perspectives, he has to develop alternative methods, equally with a sense for the long perspective of history. But under the one condition that is valid not only for theoretical activity, but for all of life.

For the hatred of the world dwells in our own hearts. It has left its marks in everything that Christians have done and thought throughout the generations. Within the given structures this hatred has run its course and left its tracks. These can only be broken up through persevering reflection and practical sacrifices. What is it that we may expect from all this?

If what we said before is true, namely, that the Christian has nothing more to obey than to follow the simple parole, then he knows his place everywhere to be *as* he finds it. From there he is to move his face forward in the direction of disclosure, to fight his battle, and to leave and hand over the result. The meaning of the battle is at the same time both very limited and without bounds. It is limited, for it is not the disciple who wages it, but the Master. For the same reason, it is without bounds.

From a human point of view, the supremacy of creational disorder by human guilt is overwhelming. It seems to leave us powerless. The more so, since the same disorder enters into everything that the Christian undertakes, both personally and in his communal organizations, pre-eminently in the organized church. It is the Master who does it all: it is His work that survives. The work of men will perish. Twice the Master meets with the disciple in his trade by the sea of Tiberius. Twice the same command is given. Then, finally, on the third occasion, after all that had gone before, the disciple understood. Is this ultimately all that creational revelation—God whom it pleased to show himself creatingly to the creature—has to say? At this point, theology and philosophy have to be silent. Here it is only the choice of faith that counts.

The answer to this question must be: Yes. That is the consequence of the cross, the consequence of God *giving* Himself. But yet, here we find ourselves, as we described before, in the root of creation, and hence in the middle of its fullness. Here we are in the focus, in the very dynamics of disclosure, our faces directed forward.

There is no other meaning for the Christian's presence on earth but to bear witness to the Master's resurrection, which is the liberation of creation. This liberation *occurs* when He comes. That is the direction of our expectation. The question as to what this means in the "practice" of life is squarely at odds with this. That question arises from a gratuitous acceptance of this faith, coupled with the idea that it only "gets meaning" when we, by means of Christian organizations, can compete with the world. Such an attitude is easily justified by the kind of "common-grace theory" that we discussed. But it expresses a diversion from the direction of true faith-disclosure. The Kingdom of Heaven, the destination of creation, is not of this world.

By all means of interpretation, the attempt has been made to escape from the emphasis of this crisis-confession by Him who was to save the world. We do it either by separating the Kingdom from the creation, and by trying to steer our own course by an appeal to a dialectical-paradoxical contradiction, or by an appeal to a difference in origin and hence in meaning between Kingdom and creation. Yet Pilate's plea was for *the* truth. Only the Kingdom, which is not of this world, gives full meaning to creation. It is impossible for man to take a stance somewhere outside of God's creative action, and from there to attempt to make a judgment about the cosmos. The best that can be expected from such an attempt are theologoumena. The only legitimate way to speak about creation is from the cross. For in cross and resurrection God's revelation has been fulfilled, and there is no way to approach its beginning but from its fulfilling center.

So, if we emphatically reject a secularized attitude as we have just presented it, we nevertheless have to maintain that the Christian's battlefield has no boundaries, no matter how sharply it is defined by the given command. The battlefield encompasses the entire cosmos. What the Christian has to do there is to *oppose* "this" world. For it is in the cosmos where the King of Truth has opposed Himself against the murderer from the beginning. Freedom over against death.

The Christian, in order to be able to oppose the world, will have to be fully acquainted with its principle and method. But such knowledge cannot be acquired by worldly methods. In the meantime, this world still "operates" by God's structures. Christ Himself bowed before them, recognizing the God-given authority and competence of His parents, His teachers, the Sanhedrin, and the Roman Praetor.

Humankind can only fulfill its creational calling in community. And the church is called to show forth the reborn community. Therefore, in principle, it will have to organize itself for its witness in the various domains of life. That will be necessary, if it is to make the witness heard that is being suppressed by the world. However, every community that it erects for this witness can only be qualified by *faith*. This marks the difference between the Christian union and every union of Christians.

This calls for a twofold distinction. A Christian organization can as such not be qualified by the areas in which it engages for battle (the state, labor, business enterprise, various areas of social intercourse, science, charity, etc.). It acts in order to give its *faith*-witness *in* those areas, according to their inner structure, in opposition to the faith-witness of the world, which has, according to the nature of the fallen world, the lead in those areas. Its witness consists in practical activity, with an aim of breaking open the bound disclosure with a newness of direction towards the truth, the new Root of creation. This activity should not be directed towards supposedly specific Christian desiderata. Such an attempt would arise from one of the aforementioned dualisms between creation and Kingdom. Rather, it should be aimed at calling *humanity* forward to the true root of life.

Only in this way can truly human, truly "creational" solidarity be realized. If carried out in this way, a rejection of "Christian" activity can only mean a denial of *the* Sacrifice of creational history. But this organization of the Christian witness cannot be an "ecclesiastical" organization in the narrow sense. The witness of the Church in every area of life is prompted by the preaching of the regenerating Word. It is this Word that preaches. And the listeners have to come together in community. This community is the specifically organized "church" ("institution"). Its offices, just as those within other witness organizations, have a specific character. They serve the *beginning* of the word of grace. This is its undeniable prerogative, and in the most pregnant sense its sovereignty within its own sphere.

Its priority is merely spiritual. It has no authority over what the Church of Christ does elsewhere. It has no earthly prerogative. It has to be like nothing in the hands of Him Who alone has authority to speak. Every act or judgment that leads away from His truth alone cancels its own competence.

The danger of secularization is just as real for the organized "church" as for the whole Christian life. The organized "church" is even the primary invasion route for secularization. Each hypostatization of "office" is a part of it, and is its primary expression. It threatens both the church's spiritual calling and its freedom of action. Naturally, it will meet with *opposition*. "Adaptation" then silences that opposition, but in effect signals the end of its true existence as church. The same holds for the organized Christian life inspired by its preaching. That life then starts to show all the marks of an army in retreat, of gradual decay, till the enemy will have rooted out the useless nominal leftovers.

But this enemy will never be able to catch *the* Church. For its King has saved creation in her. Only he who, as a member of the Body, completely takes upon himself the confession made in the face of the earthly governor, in the fullness of time, and thus holds on to the Head, may yearn for His coming—even though being in the desert. He who accepts the cross as the horizon of time will *see* the meaning of creation.

The pages of the book by which humankind will be judged are written in the disclosure of the world till the last day. Just like everybody else, the Christian is in no position to read their "letters" correctly. And the weed will continue to grow together with the wheat. Nevertheless, it is no small matter to help fill the pages of this book. What is important is *at least* to show the road of *dis*closure—according to the relevant structures and *in concreto*—to them who in spite of themselves in their stubborn closure contribute to filling the pages of this book.

It goes without saying that, in all this, people remain bound to their period and place in history. But what counts is that their labor is related to the . . . *Root* and *Origin* of creation. This Origin reveals itself in their labor and its history. Consequently, this relating is not bound to the passing of time, nor to phases of development.

This is relevant for the meeting of religious syntheses during the history of Christendom. Each new generation is bound to correct the mistakes of previous generations. But it has to be taken into account that the spirit that moved the community of some historical period moves extremely slowly. Only by much effort can it be led out onto new roads. Yet, ultimately, the spirit of the times will not be able to alienate the heart from its Origin, if it has put its fundamental trust in His word.

At the same time, this does not mean that we can be sloppy concerning the dangers that acutely threaten us in our own time. Christians who are active in "cultural" domains, and especially those of science, can be remarkably hesitant to embrace the truth of revelation. This is caused by a tendency towards secularization, in the sense of a stalling in the process of disclosure, as well as by the influence of the nature-grace motive, very often in the guise of "common grace." The warnings against "prophetism" in science have made a deep impression. And, in spite of the readiness to trust Scripture, there is also a tendency to ask about the practical utility when Scripture's principles are emphasized.

We repeatedly pointed out that the Scriptural witness has to be given in accordance with the nature of the domain of life where it has to penetrate. Otherwise it would not be a witness. What we have done in this book is to put into practice some of it for philosophy, the central area of theory and science. We concentrated on its transcendental problems.

We investigated the deeper, religious grounds of the lack of reflection. The direct and integral result of that lack of reflection is the loss of the understanding of the *reality* of religion as the *central dynamics* of human life.

The traditional idol in the theorist's structural creational domain has greatly ensnared people, so much so that all confidence is lost when an account of the possibility of theory is required. It appears to be extremely difficult to distinguish between creaturely thinking and idolized thinking. And it is equally difficult to extract one's faith from the idol, and to make one's faith direct one's thinking towards Him who claims our *complete* surrender. It appears difficult to understand that there are not two kinds of things: one kind that is only to be approached by faith, and an other kind that is only to be approached by thinking. Rather, always and everywhere, rationality only moves in the direction that faith guides it. This is the more difficult to understand when the direction of faith is towards "reason," the supposedly autonomous rationality of man.

No doubt, the road of immanent-transcendental criticism of theoretical thought (including science) is a long one. Yet, it is the only road to break up the dualism of faith and science, of nature and grace, of "prophetism" and rationality. There is no other road on which to meet the opponent at the appropriate structural point, which, because of its structural nature, he cannot avoid. It is not up to us whether he will be willing to engage us at that point. All that we have to do is to pursue him into the last corners of refuge. Then, when we have taken the trouble to get to know this road and to travel it, we are in a position to say proudly and humbly: "*For I am not ashamed of the gospel of Christ: for it is the power of God unto salvation*" [Romans 1:16, KJV]. That means the salvation of creation in all its revelational splendor, including science and theory. When its idols are done away with, in the purifying world-fire, creation, reborn by this power, will lay down its sacrifice in the *Civitas Dei*.

www.ingramcontent.com/pod-product-compliance
Lightning Source LLC
Chambersburg PA
CBHW020015050426
42450CB00005B/474